35

W9-BIQ-991

66

The Catholic
WHY?
Book

The Catholic WHY? Book

by
Andrew M. Greeley

THE THOMAS MORE PRESS
Chicago, Illinois

Second Printing

Copyright © 1983 by Andrew M. Greeley. All rights reserved. Printed in the United States of America. No part of this publication may be reproduced, stored in a retrieval system, or transmitted, in any form or by any means, electronic, mechanical, photocopying, recording, or otherwise, without the written permission of the publisher, The Thomas More Association, 225 West Huron Street, Chicago, Illinois 60610.

ISBN 0-88347-154-X

CONTENTS

The Catholic WHY? Book

1. Why am I writing this book?

This book is primarily for those Catholics who are caught between the pre-Vatican and the post-Vatican church, between the counter-reformation and the ecumenical age, people who on the one hand welcome the changes of the last twenty years, but who on the other hand were educated either before or after the council in perspectives and outlooks that no longer seem to prevail in the church.

There are a tremendous number of such people. Many of them know in their heads that the questions that gnaw at their conscience are not really the right questions but just the same they continue to gnaw, precisely because no one has rephrased the questions for them and no one has shown the link between the concern contained in the old questions and in the answers. Recently I encountered a telling example of this sort of problem which is inevitable in a church in transition. A woman who had read one of my novels during the summer told me that she had enjoyed the story enormously, but had resisted on every page the thought that priests might have erotic fantasies and temptations. A voice inside her head kept telling her, "priests can't imagine these sorts of things" or "they shouldn't imagine such things."

The woman was well educated and progressive. She KNEW that priests were human like everyone else and they are subject to all the human temptations. Sometimes some priests will give in to such temptations. In principle, she not only accepted that fact but was prepared to concede that human priests were more attractive than super-human priests who were, in fact, inhuman because they had no sense of the frailties of the human condition. But still, from the earliest years in Catholic schools, she had absorbed from her educational environment, mostly by implications, the notion that when priests took their vow of celibacy, they ceased to be "bothered" by temptations of the flesh. Priests were, she had been taught, not so much by anything that was said explicitly, but by the way everybody acted, no longer sexual beings. Until she read my novel, nothing had happened in her life to challenge this assumption or force her to update it so as to bring it into line with the post-conservative emphasis on the humanness of priests. Her head said that, of course, priests are human; her imagination resisted that possibility every inch of the way. So it is with many of us on many issues. We approve of the changes if we understand them but there are questions and problems which lurk in our memory and probe at the outer fringes of our consciousness. Often we are a little bit ashamed of these questions because we realize that they are "old church" but putting that label on them doesn't make them go away. Most of the questions that are asked in this book are "old church" questions. They assume models of the church which are no longer in frequent use. Some of them, in fact, cannot be answered because answers to them are beyond the church's capability. Most of them have to be abandoned after they have been specifically addressed. Nevertheless, Catholics cannot deal with these questions until they have at least heard them asked and then answered.

2. Why was the "old church" old?"

Those of us who were educated under pre-Vatican II influences were generally exposed to a view of Catholicism based on the following assumptions:

1. The church was perfect and so were all the leaders and policies of the Church.
2. The church had the answers to all problems. If only people would listen to those answers, the problems would go away.
3. The church also had a position on most moral and social issues. All Catholics were obliged to support those positions.
4. The properly educated Catholic was the Catholic who knew all the answers to the questions about the church that anyone might ask.
5. The most important thing in life was to "save one's soul." One did this by keeping all of the church's rules.
6. The rules were long and detailed and involved a graduated list of sins ranging from the most serious (sacrilege) to venial. Sacrileges, however, were rather rare and for most of us serious sins were sins of the "flesh." Indeed, they were just about the only sins worth worrying about. (You could really get into trouble in the old church by telling people that some sacrileges were only venial sins—which

was true but somehow or the other it didn't "seem" right.)

7. The principal danger was being sent to hell. God didn't exactly want us to go to hell but he was sternly just in keeping track of our sins and would, if need be, send us crashing down into the pit of fire even if we only committed one mortal sin in our whole life.

It was a rigid, codified, intellectualist, offensive (or apologetic) and rather merciless form of Catholicism.

3. Why were we educated that way?

For any number of reasons. The church was still in a garrison condition, fighting the Reformation with the counter-reformation. Its very existence still seemed to be in doubt. Moreover, in the United States, Catholicism was still an immigrant faith, doubly threatened by a hostile, native-born society which was mostly Protestant and American while we were Catholic and foreign. In order to protect the faith of the immigrants, it was necessary to maintain simple answers and stern discipline.

In retrospect, the threats might not have been all that serious. The faith of the immigrants was strongly protected by sociological forces. Religion was essential to immigrant identity and church leaders in that era didn't know that.

Moreover, church leaders and teachers tended to be authoritarian, both by personality and training. Clear, simple and rigid answers to all life questions met their personality needs and ideological perspective and hence had to be imposed on their people. (Incidentally, if anyone thinks that rigid ideology went with the Second Vatican Council, they haven't talked to a dedicated, radical, Catholic feminist or liberation theologian. The content of a simple moralistic answer may have changed but the style is often, alas, the same.)

Again, in retrospect, the rigidities and moralisms of immigrant Catholicism, the mixture of trium-

20

phalism and defensiveness, were probably not necessary but immigrant Catholicism did serve rather well to respond to some of the problems and crises at that time. Unfortunately, in the years after the war and before the Vatican Council, it often deteriorated into a caricature of itself. The flexibility and the pragmatism of the pioneer church gave way almost completely to a renaissance style of autocratic leadership, and absolutely unquestionable answers to every human problem. Changes in this approach would have been necessary even if there hadn't been a Second Vatican Council.

The manifestations and the incarnations of the Catholic tradition in every era are necessarily limited and imperfect. It must be said, however, that immigrant Catholicism in its declining years was very imperfect indeed. It had no sense at all of history, even though it argued vigorously about "tradition" (which often meant the way things had been done since 1920 or perhaps 1870), but it had no sense at all of the enormous variety of practices and beliefs that were part of the Catholic past nor were they willing to admit the pluralism even of the Catholic present. There was one way, and only one way. The rules might be hard but God expected us to be courageous, just like the martyrs.

Nor, in fact, were they even willing to conceive the primacy of conscience. While we may have been taught in the seminary that the ultimate norm for human behavior was the decision of conscience, there was a tendency in the immigrant, counter-reformation church not to trust the consciences of the laity and to insist that they do what we told them to do, regardless of what their conscience might say—indeed without even bothering to consult their conscience.

Finally, there were the convictions that you really couldn't trust the laity if you gave them too much freedom (because they were, after all, mostly uneducated) and the best way to motivate the laity to do those things which they were supposed to do was through fear. God's love was honored in principle, but in practice the main motivation for human goodness was fear.

Moreover, virtue was thought to be developed by forcing people to do things that were good for them. Thus, young people were supposed to learn the habit of frequent confession by being forced to go to confession on the Thursday before First Friday. It was the rare pastor or curate who did not think that it was a good idea to herd all the children attending school over to church on the Thursday morning before First Friday and process them through the confessionals as, in a later era, cards would be processed through a computer. "They learn good habits that way" was the justification for such behavior. (If a pastor occasionally felt the need he had to justify anything he did). Now this approach was utterly foreign to the Catholic tradition which holds with Thomas Aquinas that virtue was acquired not by compulsion but by the repetition of FREE acts. If a curate dared to quote St. Thomas, the pastor's response was either to say "I'm the pastor and will do it my way" or to argue that St. Thomas wasn't dealing with immigrants whose faith was being threatened by a hostile native-American environment.

Any incarnation in time and place of the Catholic vision is bound to be a bit of a caricature, but the Catholicism in which many of us were raised was, in retrospect, a very bad caricature during its final years. We may feel angry about that but the anger doesn't do much good. The men and women who drummed the simplest, moralistic rigidities of that era into our heads were sincere and dedicated. They thought they were forcing us to be virtuous or scaring us to be virtuous for our own good. They were wrong, profoundly wrong. They never even enjoyed authoritarian power but their ignorance, to use the word of which they were fond, was invincible.

The point for us today is that we ought not to confuse the narrow and rigid and insensitive version of the Catholic tradition with the tradition itself.

4. Why does the church insist that we all worship God in the same way?

It doesn't.

There are many different styles of spirituality within the Catholic tradition—Jesuit, Franciscan, Benedictine, for example—and many different kinds of prayer and devotion. Moreover, even at Mass there are in fact many different ways in which people can participate and indeed different parishes now have different liturgical styles and occasionally one can find masses that are celebrated in the old Latin version. Moreover, the church does not deny the validity of Protestant or Jewish or non-Christian or even pagan worship. Indeed, the Catholic Mass, based as it is on the Jewish Passover service, which in its turn is based on pagan spring festivals, has absorbed many different religious traditions. Catholicism no longer claims that it has a total monopoly on religious truth or valid worship. It does not believe that one religion is as good as another and it does believe (and its tradition most fully and most adequately reflects) the teaching of Jesus, but it does not renounce or repudiate other traditions.

5. Why can only priests say Mass?

The priest doesn't "say Mass" anymore; he presides over the Eucharistic assembly. This is more than just a trendy phrase. It indicates rather that the whole Christian community worships God at Mass and the priest is the one who is designated from among the community to lead the worship. Everyone offers Mass together with the president of the assembly. Mass is no longer a private devotion mumbled by the priest upon the altar while the congregation watches in awed and bemused silence from a distance. It is their worship ceremony, offered by the whole community, each member of which participates in his or her own way.

6. Why doesn't watching Mass on television fulfill our Sunday obligation?

First of all, some historians of moral theology argue that the precept of Sunday obligation created by the Lateran Council was never intended to bind under the pain of serious sin.

If one can't go to Mass any other way, then participation through television is certainly an excellent aid to Sunday devotion. However, the television participant is really not physically present with the rest of the community when worship is offered, anymore than somebody who "attends" a meal from a great distance through closed circuit television can be said to be physically present. When the president addresses a fund-raising dinner through closed circuit television, it is certainly nice for the party faithful to watch him and hear him, but nobody would seriously contend that the president had eaten dinner with the people at the banquet.

7. Why is the church so strict on sexual morality but so lenient on materialism?

I'm not sure what you mean by materialism. If you mean the enjoyment of the material goods of this world, then the church can't be strict on the subject because there is nothing wrong with enjoying material possessions so long as they don't dominate our lives.

Furthermore, the church has been pretty severe on the abuses of material possessions. Indeed, Pope John Paul denounces "consumerism" in most of his speeches, equating Western consumerism with Eastern Communism. (Quite unfairly, it seems to me. Consumerism, whatever its faults, does not abolish free trade unions like Solidarity.) The proper use of material goods, however, is normally a decision that must be made by the individual in the free exercise of conscience. What is proper for one person in one set of circumstances might not be proper for someone else.

The principles of sexual morality seem to be much clearer and more precise and more universal, at least in theory. Nonetheless, sexual sins are not the only sins or the worst sins. Jesus spent relatively little of his time on matters of sexual morality. To the extent that church leaders and teachers permit themselves to become obsessed by sexual sins and ignore all others, they are simply not being faithful to their own tradition.

8. If the New Testament superseded the Old, why do we still use it?

To begin with, it might be more appropriate if one uses the terms "Jewish Scriptures" and "Christian Scriptures" for many Jewish people, not without reason, find the term "Old Testament" somewhat offensive. Moreover, Christian Scriptures do not at all supersede the Jewish Scriptures; they rather continue, develop and fulfill the Jewish Scriptures. There is one plan of salvation history, not two. The God who revealed himself to Adam and Moses and Jacob and David is the same God who revealed himself to us through Jesus. There is a continuity of revelation, of themes and even of ceremony in the Jewish and Christian Scriptures. In most languages, for example, the spring festival has the same name—pascha (Easter is in fact an Anglo-Saxon pagan name, celebrating the feast of "Eastern," the Anglo-Saxon goddess of the dawn and of spring—whose symbols, by the way, were lillies, bunnies and eggs). An anthropologist from another planet would think that Christianity and Judaism were two sects both derived from Judaism, temporarily separated perhaps, but still very much part of a common religious strain. Jesus did not intend to form a church which would be distinct from Judaism. Early Christianity was rather one of the many religious movements within the pluralistic religious culture of second temple Judaism. The split between synagogue and temple was a tragic misfortune which eventually in God's providence will be undone.

9. Why have popular devotions almost disappeared?

Have you been to any charismatic meetings lately? If you have, why do you say popular devotions have disappeared? In fact, most of those things which were called popular devotions weren't all that popular. People had stopped saying the rosary, stopped attending benediction, stopped making the Stations of the Cross. The Vatican Council changes simply gave parish priests an excuse for terminating the devotions in which most people were no longer interested. And the people were no longer interested because these devotions did not respond to their religious needs. The Christmas crib is still very much present, grace is still said before meals, and May crownings are coming back into fashion. As the elitists within the church are beginning to discover, Mary, the Mother of Jesus, is a resource and an asset instead of a liability. Old popular devotions die, new popular devotions appear and some popular devotions which pseudo-sophisticates think are no longer important have remarkable durability.

10. Why are there no longer miracles?

Didn't the sun rise this morning? Don't little children toddle down the street? Don't people still love you? Are there not still stars in the heaven? Do not reconciliations occur after bitter quarrels? What do you mean miracles no longer occur? If you mean wonderful events, particularly healing events of the sort which are recounted in the New Testament, they still do occur,it would seem, occasionally. The proper attitude for Christians towards such events, however, is the attitude of St. Mark who wrote his Gospel to refute stories that attempted to turn Jesus into a worker of miracles and nothing else. Mark downplayed the miracles, put them into context and warned about those who have an insatiable passion for signs and wonders. Jesus did heal, Mark concedes, but he was not at all primarily a healer. He was rather a teacher and storyteller who came to reveal the power of God's love; the healings he accomplished were not proofs nor where they spectacles to titillate curiosity. They were merely signs of the great power of God's healing love. Unfortunately, those who have passionate appetites for private revelations and miracles do not seem to grasp St. Mark's point.

11. Why is moral theology so far behind reality?

Mostly, I suspect, because moral theologians are academics and academics, perhaps necessarily, are generally pretty far removed from reality. It also requires considerable time and effort to understand the complex problems of, let us say, genetic engineering. By the time the moral theologians have been able to comprehend the issues first raised when the scientists began combining various DNA elements, the scientific community had already established that the fears initially raised about this behavior were groundless. The moral theologians had their perspectives on the questions ready for distribution when the questions had already been answered (and most the fears raised, incidentally, had turned out to have been more a matter of political ideology than of scientific understanding.) There is nothing much that can be done about this gap unless you want moral theologians to shoot their mouths off without understanding the issues involved in complex, modern, ethical problems (and heaven knows that there are not a few moral theologians who are only too willing to do that). It also should be understood that in matters of sexual morality, moral theologians take very considerable risks if they try to engage in any development of Catholic positions. Some church leaders seem to think that if you can silence moral theologians, you can brow-beat the laity into doing what they are told. There isn't much chance of that working, of course, but there are not very many people that bishops can push around anymore and moral theologians happen to be an excellent target for the needs that some hierarchs have for pushing people around.

12. Why must priests stay out of politics?

I didn't notice that they are staying out of politics. The Marxist government in Nicaragua, for example, has several priests as cabinet ministers. The so-called ban on priests' participation in politics was nothing more than a ploy by the American Right To Life Movement to get rid of Congressman Bob Drinan, a ploy which the Vatican and the Jesuit order, to their shame, accepted. The prohibition hasn't been applied to anyone else.

Pope John Paul II clearly doesn't like priests involved in politics. He argues that in the proper division of roles, politics is the role of the laity and preaching the gospel and developing the laity's religious resources so they can participate effectively is the priests' role. To tell you the truth, I agree with the Pope. Most priests who get involved in politics are clearly on a clerical discount expecting the Roman collar and their religious commitment to make up for their lack of knowledge and sophistication. As Father John Carroll (who went on to become the first American bishop) said, most priests are not very good politicans because they lack the skills and understandings required for political life. Moreover, it is the goal of the politician to build coalitions around broad consensuses which frequently are based on compromise solutions with which all members of the coalition can live; whereas a religious leader urges, not compromise, but idealism and generosity. Unfortunately, when many priests become politicans, they must choose the skills and behaviors that are appropriate for politics. There is always fanaticism, rigid, unbending ideology which demands that everyone accept the priests-politicians as perfectionists. Some men (and some women) may be able to combine the two sets of skills, but such combinations are rare. The priest-politician is often a poor politician, and not infrequently also becomes a poor priest or even leaves the priesthood altogether because he finds that politics are more fun.

While I agree with John Carroll that the clergy ought to stay out of politics, I do not want to make such a prohibition absolute because there are sometimes situations where it is essential for priests to become politically involved. But I think the proper posture for clergy is to leave politics to the laity, except in those cases where as a matter of last resort the presence of the clergy is absolutely essential. Such cases, it seems to me, are few and far between.

13. Why is the church so legalistic and judgmental when Jesus wasn't?

Probably because the church is a large corporate bureaucracy and bureaucrats tend to be legalistic and judgmental. It's also easier to make, enforce and even obey laws than to respond to the kind of passionate and demanding love which Jesus revealed. By keeping rules, we deal with God and dealing with God, bargaining with him, and even compromising with him is not nearly so threatening as loving him and accepting his love. However, to the extent that the church has become so legalistic that it has forgotten about the love that Jesus revealed, it has failed to be what it ought to be.

14. Why doesn't the Pope outlaw war?

The Pope is a religious leader, the bishop of Rome, the presiding bishop of all the bishops of the world. He has a hard enough time persuading his own staff and other bishops to do what he wants them to do. How could he possibly persuade the political leaders of the world, to say nothing of the people of the world, most of whom are not Catholic, that war is wrong—especially when some kinds of war in self-defense may very well not be wrong. The question seems to want the Pope to identify pacifism with Christian doctrine, but in fact all pacifism is is a legitimate Christian option. It simply is not the only option within the heritage. The right of self-defense is still a basic human right that the Pope can't take away. Obviously the Pope can and should (and often has) plead for peace, do everything in his power to prevent war, attempt to mitigate the horrors of war when they occur and beg Christians and Christian leaders to take the lead in promoting disarmament to prevent war. But the Pope's power, even religiously, is not absolute and the notion that he is some kind of vice-regent to God who can outlaw anything he wants simply won't stand up either to a Catholic heritage or to common sense.

15. Why are some actions sinful if they hurt no one?

This is just as good a place as any to assert bluntly that the church is not in the ethics business. The church's task is to teach religion; that is to say, to reveal the nature of God and the purpose of human life. Jesus was not primarily an ethical teacher at all—despite what you may have heard. He was a religious visionary, a storyteller of God, a man with a passionate insight into the power of God's love. The church's principal job is to keep that insight alive, to share it with other human beings and to pass it on from generation to generation. There are ethical conclusions which follow from the religious insight of Jesus, and Jesus himself did indeed draw these ethical conclusions but he did not expound a systematic ethic, much less a moral theology. To the extent that the church permits itself to become so engrossed with ethics and moral theology (either of the right wing or the left) and forgets its fundamental obligation to proclaim the religious vision of Jesus, it fails in its basic task.

Now, having said these things one must say that actions are sinful because they do violence to human nature and not merely because the church says they are sinful. Sometimes the harm that a person does to himself or to another through a sin might not be immediately obvious. "Well, we are living together with one another but we know what we are doing and we are not going to hurt each other" is not an infrequent claim. But how can anyone know that such people are not going to hurt one another or that the relationship is not going to be a harmful one even though it may not appear so to two people engaged in it. Normally the thing which "doesn't hurt anybody" is an act of perhaps unintentional self-deception.

16. Why can't women become priests?

I'm not the one to answer this because I simply do not believe the arguments against women priests; but the arguments that one hears are as follows:

Jesus was a man. Jesus didn't choose any women to be his apostles. The church has never had women priests. The symbolism of the Eucharist requires that a man preside over it.

Candidly, I think these are rotten arguments. Jesus did not ordain priests in the sense that we ordain them. He merely gathered followers and entrusted them with a mission of organizing his community. In the Palestinian Judaism of his time, the culture was sufficiently patriarchal that the question of women presiding over the Eucharist simply did not and could not occur (though the attitude of Jesus towards women, his respect and affection for them, the fairness of his treatment of them was so remarkable that by themselves they might constitute a powerful argument that Jesus was no mere human being). It is not clear that women have not presided over the Eucharistic assembly at various times in Christian history. Indeed, there are some traces of evidence available that suggest they have on occasion been Eucharistic presidents and even perhaps bishops. Obvious and sometimes true attempts have been made to cover up these historical phenomena. The argument about male symbolism in the Eucharist is a mish-mash of nonsense, as are most arguments based on symbols that are made by theologians and church leaders who do not understand what a complex, dense, multi-layered and polyvalent thing a symbol is.

My own feeling is that opposition to women priests comes from the profound male chauvinism of many church leaders born of the fear that any changes, particularly such a drastic change, will be an enormous threat to the power of the Roman curia. Indeed, it is a good rule of thumb that when anyone advances problematic, theological and symbolic reasons to oppose a change, the real issue isn't theology at all but organizational power. Finally, many if not most men fear women. Priests and bishops are no different from any others. Indeed, some church leaders are clearly sexually neutered, do not like women, do not find them attractive, try to avoid them whenever possible, and would find their whole being threatened if they had to share the ministry with women.

On the other hand, I'm not altogether sure that women in the priesthood will improve the church anymore than the women's vote improved politics. It is a change which I think right and just, but not one which finally is going to make all that much difference in what the church is.

17. Why is there so little about Mary in the New Testament?

Probably because the New Testament writers didn't realize that devotion to Mary, the Mother of Jesus, was going to be developed and become so important in the early New Testament church. In any event, they were interested especially in the problems of the community for which they were writing and each of the four evangelists had a specific perspective of his audience in mind, a perspective which had to do basically with the life and the nature of Jesus. Mary simply wasn't on their agenda, and trying to put her on their agenda is reading back into those times questions and issues which did not then exist. Admittedly, the search in the New Testament for answers to contemporary problems is something in which almost everybody seems to engage, but that doesn't make it intellectually or religiously legitimate.

18. Why does the church still seem to take seriously Paul's put-down of women?

Paul was not as much a feminist as Jesus and yet, compared to most men of his era, he was extraordinarily enlightened. Indeed, in one of his Epistles, he denies the importance of a distinction between male and female (and between Jew and Gentile) in the Christian church, thus opting for a fundamental equality between men and women, an equality which was virtually unheard of in his time. If church leaders continue to put down women—and they do, intolerably and inexcusably in my judgment—the reason is not St. Paul but, as I said in response to an earlier question, their own chauvinism and their own fear of women—a chauvinism and fear on which they have no monopoly. It is also worth noting that despite the injustices against women in the church, they also have more check-signing power in Catholicism than they do in almost any corporate organization in the world, and more administrative clout too, for that matter.

19. Why don't the cardinals of the church practice poverty?

Why should they? Poverty is one of the so-called evangelical counsels, a particular style of life that is an option not an obligation. An option to which not everyone is called and which, while it may be linked with the religious life and the monastic life, is by no means necessarily linked to priestly ordination. A secular priest and a cardinal have the same obligation to generosity (a better word than "poverty") as do all baptized lay people; that is to say, a very serious and weighty obligation indeed, to use their extra money wisely and generously in the service of other humans. But a cardinal has no more obligation to poverty from his priestly office or his papal dignity than does any baptized member of any parish in the world. In fact, despite the fancy robes, many of the cardinals live very modestly indeed. Their salary ($8,000 per year the last time I checked on it) is meager and while many of them have other sources of income, many of them do not. I've occasionally been in cardinals' apartments and they are neither luxurious nor lavish, and their toilet facilities are no more reliable than any others in Italy.

I think there is a kind of hypocrisy in questions like this. Jesus, after all, said "judge not that you be not judged," and while there are perhaps some kinds of extraordinarily lavish lifestyles that might not be appropriate for church leaders, few church-men live this way anymore, and the way they do live ought to be between them and God, not a sub-ject of hypocritical and envious sneering on the part of the laity. Thus, when Archbishop Bernardin came to Chicago, an idiot wrote a letter to the *National Catholic Reporter* arguing that he should ride public transportation, eat at hot dog stands, and drive his own car—as though these were the really important things that a new archbishop had to do, and as though most of them were not window-dressing and grandstanding, an inap-propriate waste of the archbishop's time and energy which might more practically be devoted to other goals.

20. Why is it necessary to gather together to pray?

It isn't really necessary. Obviously, we can pray by ourselves. We come to pray in the Eucharistic assembly because we are social animals, not solitary creatures like cougars. Most human activities are social activities. We do them with others, so it is perfectly natural and normal that some of the time we come together to pray. Community worship reinforces our faith, strengthens our hope, validates our courage, and helps us to go forth from these interludes of prayer together stronger, more generous and more loving humans.

21. Why is marriage a permanent state?

To begin with, marriage is not permanent because the church says it is. Rather, the church says that marriage is permanent because there is a fundamental propensity towards permanence in human sexual relationships, a propensity programmed into our species millions of years ago as a necessary precondition for our evolution into homosapiens. Our proto- and pre-hominid ancestors had to develop sexual love in the family before evolution could get anywhere near us. Humans are "quasi-pairbonded"; not as pairbonded as certain species of birds, for example, but nonetheless held together by sexual attraction which is pervasive (unlike any other mammal species) so that the male and the female may stay together long enough to rear their children into adulthood. If there is one finding of contemporary anthropology and social biology that utterly confirms the church's teaching it is the propensity to permanence in the bond between husband and wife. This bond, you see, does not come from the marriage contract or even from the sacramentality of the union. Quite the contrary, the contract ratifies and the sacrament celebrates the union by which two become one flesh which was built into the human condition long before we were able to think of contracts or imagine sacraments. A relationship between a man and a woman which does not have a propensity toward permanence or in which this propensity is resisted or denied does grave violence to the essence of human nature. Marriage is permanent not because it reflects sacramentally the union between Christ and his church; rather it reflects the unity between Christ and his church precisely because of the powerful strain in human nature towards permanent bonding of a man and a woman who have sex with one another. Obviously, the propensity can be resisted, but equally obviously sometimes the bond is not strong enough to become irresistibly permanent. But the permanence is there, part of the physical, biological, psychological and genetic programming of human nature.

It must be understood, however, that the church has defended the propensity to permanence in marriage in many different ways in its history. Thus, in the 6th century, St. Boniface and St. Gregory corresponded about the various circumstances in which remarriage could be permitted if one's spouse was still alive—if the spouse was missing at sea or in war, one of the partners had leprosy, one of the partners was freed from slavery, etc., etc. For the first thousand years of church history, there were no specific ecclesiastical regulations for marriage. Indeed, there was no explicitly liturgical ceremony. The church simply honored the civil legislation and the civil marriage ceremony, and while many will deny (and perhaps with some plausibility) that the church has changed its teaching on divorce in recent years, it is nonetheless true that, practically speaking, the present annulment processes, grounded in sound psychology incidentally, represent a dramatic change in the attitudes towards divorce and remarriage which had until very recently held sway.

22. Why is the church so much more lenient on annulments today?

The leniency comes from a deeper understanding of human psychology. Granting the propensity towards permanence in human pairbonding, the church nonetheless realizes that many people who marry are not sufficiently sure to contract the kind of permanent union which indeed does represent and reflect the union between Christ and the church (and thus is sacramental). Implicit in this practice is the hint that it takes a while in many marriages (some would say most marriages) for the union to become sufficiently deep, sufficiently mature and sufficiently committed for it to be a sacrament, and when that happens dissolubility is no longer an issue because however much the strain and the conflict, the spouses would never think of leaving one another. In any case, the new grounds for annulment basically come from a deeper understanding of psychological immaturity and a fuller realization of how immature many, if not most, people are when they enter the marriage state. (The new code of Canon Law (1983), however, tightens and limits some of the grounds, as well as re-establishing universal tribunal hearings.)

23. **Why should the dead who have someone to pray for them have an advantage over those who have no one to pray for them?**

Aw, come on, you don't really believe that kind of stuff, do you?

You don't really think God plays the game that way, do you?

If you do, go back and read the New Testament.

Anyway, purgatory is not so much a place for expiating sins as a place for straightening out the messed up relationships of our lives. The prayers for the "poor souls" of us here on earth may well help that work (so marvelously described in the final chapter of D. M. Thomas' novel, *The White Hotel*) that I think we can trust God to see that the prayers and their effects are fairly distributed.

Andrew M. Greeley

24. Why do a lot of smart people not believe in God?

A lot of smart people do believe in God, but so what? Faith is not a matter of intelligence and certainly not the kind of intelligence that leads people to obtain Ph.D.'s (which is often a very rigid, unimaginative and self-deceiving kind of intelligence—I know, I have a Ph.D.!).

Faith is not so much a matter of intelligence as it is docility to the signs of grace that abound all around us in the world, an openness to the influence of God as God reveals himself in the works of nature and in the human beings who love us. A good many smart people, often including those who have Ph.D.'s, are simply insensitive to wonder and giftedness. They may be very brilliant in their own areas of specialization, but about everything else in the world they are still sophomores.

It is also true that some of those who, for one reason or another, are religiously alienated turned to scholarship as a substitute for religion. Certain kinds of academic disciplines seem to selectively recruit those who are alienated from God and church in faith and heritage (including, sad to say, sociology).

Finally, many of those smart people who do not believe in God in fact reject the caricatures of God that were imposed on them during very rigid religious upbringing (and fundamentalist Protestants and hyper-orthodox Jews were far more rigid than preconciliar Catholics). Such men and women may have turned against the God that they knew, but in their commitment to goodness and generosity honor, without realizing it, a God they do not know because they live and act as if there were indeed graciousness in the universe. Such an acknowledgment of graciousness is, practically speaking, the same thing as belief in God. To put the matter differently, the God in whom they were taught to believe is not a God in whom it is worth believing. Even God himself would reject that kind of God.

25. Why am I afraid to die when I believe in God and have lived a good life?

You are afraid to die because death is the cracking apart of your personality, the separation of life from your body, the withering and corruption of mortal flesh that is laid in the ground. That's scary regardless of what you believe. Even Jesus, during his agony in the garden, was afraid to die. You may very well believe in God, but you've never seen him. And you may very well believe in the life which is to come, but you've never been there. You are setting sail on an unknown voyage to a land that you rather think might be on the other side but about whose existence you are not sure the way you are sure of the existence of the house across the street. Anybody in their right mind is afraid of death, though many people, perhaps most, in the very last moments of their life seem to lose their fear, and those who have been resuscitated after being pronounced dead or who have gone through near-death experiences seem pretty much to lose their fear of death. As Bob Fosse tells us in his remarkable film, *All That Jazz*, death, when finally encountered, seems gracious, benign, lovely, gentle, affectionate, tender—almost like a lover.

26. Why did the church rescind its ban on charging interest?

The standard answer is that the church revised its teaching on interest because in the economy of the late middle ages and early Renaissance, the nature of money underwent a profound change. Instead of being a static resource, money became dynamic: that is to say, capable of being invested so as to earn income. The person who had to borrow money in the previous era was usually a farmer or a merchant who was near destitution because of a natural disaster. The one who borrowed money later on was the man who was going to put it to productive uses to earn more money—the investor. The changing productivity of money, in other words, changed the nature of lending from exploitation (usury) to investment.

This explanation seems adequate though, in fact, there was probably a lot of investment—and a lot of interest-charging too—before the official change.

The important point is that of course the church changed some of the more periferal elements in its teachings as social, economic, political and familial circumstances changed and as the church progressed in its understanding both of God's love and of the moral law. However, one must keep in mind what I said in response to an earlier question. The church is not primarily in the ethics business, although it is the custodian of an ancient ethical heritage which it absorbed from the Greek and Roman and Jewish worlds. The confusion of religion—a response to God's love—and systematic ethical norms is a problem that will continue to plague the church until the distinction is made sharply and clearly.

27. Why do we pray "and lead us not into temptation," which would seem to imply that God lures us to evil?

Oh, come on now! Whatever the words say, God doesn't lead us into evil. You ought to know that. "Protect us from the pass of temptation" might be a better translation. But this ought to be obvious to anyone. Unfortunately one of the many weaknesses of immigrant Catholicism was a mindless literalness which seemed to suggest that we do not use our common sense in trying to understand religious truth.

28. Why have so many priests and nuns abandoned their vocations?

First of all, we must say that most priests and most nuns have not abandoned their vocations. The majority have remained loyal. Indeed, for priests, the resignation rate is substantially lower than the divorce rate for Catholic marriages.

Most of those who left the priesthood (and I can speak with confidence on this subject because of research my colleagues and I at the National Opinion Research Center have done) were simply not happy in doing the work of priests. In the absence of happiness in one's work, the loneliness of the celibate life becomes intolerable. It is worth noting that the majority of them would not return to the priesthood even if they could do so as married priests, and only 20 percent of them would return to the work they had been doing if they could do so as married priests. (The others would want weekend work or specialized kinds of work). Thus 80 percent of the resigned priests are really not interested in going back to the sort of work they had been doing. Were men and women any less unhappy in their religious life before the Second Vatican Council? I doubt it. But the Council and the subsequent changes in the church, as well as the vacilitating and erratic but nonetheless authentic sympathy of Pope Paul VI for unhappy priests, made it much easier for priests to obtain dispensations, and once it became easy canonically to leave the priesthood, it was discovered that lay people were sympathetic towards resigned priests, not hostile, and that even the families of resigned priests could accept their resignation with some equanimity. So, when more recently, dispensations became harder to get, the attitude in the Catholic community toward the resigned priest continues to be sympathetic and many men will leave the priesthood and marry even though they do not have a dispensation because they feel that God and the Catholic community will be sympathetic and tolerant even if the papacy is not.

On the whole, even though I sometimes feel abandoned when a priest I know leaves the active ministry, I guess I have to say that both the church and the person are better off and that keeping men in the priesthood who are fundamentally and profoundly unhappy is no help to the service of human-kind or the preaching of the gospel.

Where the church and the religious orders might be to blame for some of the unhappiness in the men and women who elect to leave is, I think, a very important question. Clearly the religious life, for example, was extremely constrained and indeed sometimes intolerably oppressive for many women. The constraints and the oppressions have little to do with Christianity and indeed were, if anything, in violation of the spirit of the gospel. It is not clear, however, whether the hasty reforms in the religious communities after the Vatican Council were an adequate response to these problems. Indeed, the changes made may have done more harm than good and may have thrown the baby out with the bath water—though, as an outsider to the religious life, I cannot say this for certain. Surely the feudal domination of curates by pastors was a horrendous situation which the church tolerated far too long (and to some extent still tolerates today), and the autocratic Renaissance Monarch Bishop, though a vanishing breed, also made many men's lives virtually intolerable. Without wishing to take away the personal responsibility of those who elect to leave the priesthood or religious life, I nonetheless must say that I think their resignations are a judgment on the institutional church for its inability to make the priesthood and the religious life much more livable than they were and to some extent still are.

29. Why did Peter and Paul clash in the early church?

They clashed because they had a difference of opinion—certainly not the last difference of opinion among church leaders. The issue was the extent to which pagan converts to Christianity were obliged to obey the Jewish law. It was not nearly as simple a question as it may seem today, because Judaism was a vast religious culture and not a specific "denomination" like it is at present and Christianity was one of the many religious movements within Judaism. It was not, therefore, clear to many of the early Jewish Christians how you could be a Christian and at the same time not be a Jew. Peter and Paul agreed in principle that the Gentile converts did not have to become Jews in order to become Christians, but Paul was more willing than Peter to translate this theory into practice because the latter, working mostly with Jewish Christians as he was, was sensitive to the weakness of their understandings and tried to avoid shocking them. Paul was the man of principle and Peter the man of compromise, in substantial part, because of the context in which they found themselves. We only have Paul's account of the confrontation and he claims that he won, which surely in terms of the historical facts, he did, because his view of the problem became church policy. In all likelihood, however, the solution was not quite so clear-cut and like many other differences of opinion among church leaders, was probably settled through a compromise with which both men could live.

The Peter-Paul conflict, however, is nicely paradigmatic of future conflicts in the church. Two men of good will and good faith and good intentions differed on a matter of crucial policy importance, not because one man was good and the other was bad but because the two saw the problem from different perspectives because they worked in different contexts. The controversy also illustrated how ridiculous is the pious wish of certain of the devout faithful that there be no differences of opinion or disagreements between church leaders. As long as there are different perspectives and different contexts, different points of view and different angles to problems, there will be such differences of opinion, and sometimes, indeed frequently, acrimony. Charity does not eliminate the differences of opinion. It rather motivates the leaders involved to find solutions with which all sides can live. Charity, in other words, is not the art of repressing differences, but rather the art of finding creative compromises.

30. Why do we believe that the laws of nature can be changed by prayer?

I really wasn't aware that we did believe it. If you mean the prayers of petition for a sick person, say someone who is diagnosed as terminally ill with cancer, are a petition that the laws of nature be changed, I would simply deny that that's what the prayers mean. The prayers are rather a plea for God's mercy and for God's love and perhaps a plea that in his mercy and love, and if it be his will and be for the good of all involved, the cancer might go into a state of remission. If one means that sometimes in prayer we are asking literally for a "miracle" in which the laws of nature are suspended, the issue becomes a little more complex. However, even in a miracle, there is no real evidence that the laws of nature are changed. Whatever happens, happens in accordance with the law of nature, but through processes and dynamisms and mechanisms we don't fully understand. Any good physician, however, will tell you that the so-called laws of nature are not as hard or rigid or as mathematical as some positivistic scientists would have you believe. There is a lot of uncertainty, flexibility, unpredictability, and even mystery about the way nature works. Within that mystery there is very considerable room for surprise—and I suspect that's all most people pray for, a surprise which manifests the wonder of God's love. I fail to see that there's anything wrong with praying for a surprise as long as we realize that it is up to God, since this is his universe, to decide how the surprises are going to work.

31. Why are people suffering in hell or purgatory because they ate meat on Friday in the old days?

Do you really think that God sends people to hell for eating meat on Friday? If you do, go back and read the Scriptures, in particular the parables of Jesus. I can't help it that we were taught that eating meat on Friday was a mortal sin. Maybe it was and maybe it wasn't. One of the nasty things about preconciliar Catholicism was its propensity to multiply mortal sins so the whole environment was littered with them. Nevertheless, it's sad to say an immigrant, preconciliar Catholicism could manage to develop, quite contrary to the Catholic heritage under the Scriptures, the picture of a God who was vigorously determined, indeed almost pathologically eager, to send us off to hell. That is simply not the way God is and we should have known better even then.

32. Why is the theologian, Schillebeeckx, in disfavor with the Vatican?

Mostly because he had the misfortune of being a seminary rival of Archbishop Hamer who is the "evil genius" of the Holy Office (or the Congregation for the Defense of the Faith, as the Inquisition is now euphemistically called). It is important to realize that much of the persecution of theologians that still occurs in the Church has little to do with doctrine and much to do with personal rivalry, envy, and the Roman Curia's insatiable need for power. The difference between Schillebeeckx's case and the case of the Swiss Theologian, Hans Kung, is that Schillebeeckx had the Dutch hierarchy behind him (in the person of Cardinal Jan Gorge Willebrands) and Kung lacked the support of the German cardinals (indeed, the German cardinals were explicitly and specifically out to get him—with the same ingenuity and sensitivity with which the Germans won the Second World War). The Schillebeeckx case then can be seen as a power struggle between the Curia and Willebrands which Willebrands won, as local hierarchies normally do when they stand by their own men. The way the Vatican Inquisition works can be illustrated by some of the details of Schillebeeckx's case: he did not have a detailed list of the charges against him, he was not told who his "defense" attorney would be, and the day before the trial one of his judges announced Schillebeeckx's guilt on Vatican Radio—all violations of fundamental human rights which make the Pope's plea for the honoring of human rights in institutions outside the church look, at best, insensitive and, at worst, hypocritical.

The actual charges against Father Schillebeeckx were that his books on christology were not sufficiently orthodox. By this it was meant not that he had taught anything at odds with church tradition, but that his "christology from below" did not sufficiently repeat and emphasize the doctrinal formulations of the past. Obviously this "omission" is a vague and amorphous charge, especially since other theologians more popular with the Romans (such as Walter Kasper) have in their "christologies from below" said virtually the same thing as Father Schillebeeckx and were not charged with sins of omission.

Most theologians think of Schillebeeckx's christology as thoroughly and completely orthodox, although not all of them, even the most progressive, would necessarily agree with the details of his position (they would not think the details were heterodox, however). Thus, the great American theologian, David Tracy, has some rather pointed criticisms of Schillebeeckx's position, but Tracy's criticisms scarcely imply Schillebeeckx is not a paragon of orthodoxy.

The issue clearly then is not doctrine but power.

Andrew M. Greeley

The Roman Curia is frightened of anyone in the Catholic world who seems to have influence and who is not completely under its thumb, especially when the someone is an old rival from seminary days. The persecution of Edward Schillebeeckx is a scandal and a disgrace of which the church and the Curia ought to be heartily ashamed.

33. Why did the church wait until the 19th century to declare as doctrines Papal Infallibility and the Immaculate Conception?

That is a very good question and there are not a few Catholic thinkers who believe that there is no need to declare such doctrines. However, in the 19th century, it did appear to many churchmen that such exercise of papal and magisterial power were an effective response to the arrogance of agnostic liberalism which dominated the intellectual life of Europe (and which since has been rejected even more fully by contemporary thinkers than it was in the 19th century by the church). Nonetheless, the reign of Pio Nono does not, in retrospect, seem to be an era in which the church ought to take such pride. While those Catholic writers who suggested that Vatican I was an invalid council may have gone too far, it is also clear that there was not nearly as much freedom of discussion as there might have been.

Oddly enough, papal infallibility seems now only to be a theorctical issue. While Hans Kung got himself into deep trouble by addressing the issue, it does not seem likely that, practically speaking, any Pope is going to exercise the prerogative of infallibility—whatever it may mean—in the years ahead. And while the symbolic role of Mary, the Mother of Jesus, is (as our empirical research demonstrates) as important as ever to young Catholics and also appealing to young non-Catholics, the doctrine of the Immaculate Conception does not seem to have all that much to do with the importance of Mary in the contemporary church.

None of this is to suggest that either doctrine is not part of the body of Catholic belief, but merely to indicate that the issues aren't nearly as important today as they seemed to be in 1870.

34. Why are there so few lay, particularly married, saints?

Mostly, I suspect, because lay people and married people don't found religious orders, or are not members of religious orders, and the canonization process requires a sustained commitment of time, energy and finance. While the process of canonization may make some intellectual sense (and the regulations drawn up by Pope Clement are very wise indeed in their caution and strength), it might be permissible to wonder today whether the whole canonization mechanism might be a little bit too baroque for our time. Saints are supposed to be men and women who provide models for our lives. It is not immediately clear if those folks who are processed through the canonization apparatus today really provide that much in the way of practical modeling for ordinary Christians. It may be that the old process in which one became a saint more or less by popular acclamation might be more appropriate (and all sainthood means is that the person's virtues are worthy of imitation). In any case, even if the present canonization mechanisms continue, it is still necessary to find some other way to provide role models for the laity and, in particular, for the married laity.

However, for whatever consolation it may bring, Peter, the first Bishop of Rome, was a married man and that did not prevent him from being a saint.

He didn't belong to a religious order either.

35. Why isn't the washing of feet as much a part of the Eucharistic Liturgy as the other traditional Last Supper elements?

I don't know whether you mean the Holy Thursday Liturgy or the Sunday Liturgy. I think most parishes still either actually wash the feet or do some modern equivalent of it on Holy Thursday. As for ordinary daily Mass, many of the elements of the Last Supper Seder are omitted. We don't eat herbs or the pascal lamb, either, though indeed the Eucharist is a repetition of the Passover festival.

Anyway, most Sunday masses take long enough as it is, what with the traffic jams in the parking lots of contemporary Catholic parishes. It might be much wiser for those advocates of liturgical reform to improve the deplorable quality of most lay readings of the first two lessons at Mass than to institute compulsively historical modifications like a weekly washing of feet.

& IMPROVE LOUSY SERMONS

36. Why can some consummated marriages be annulled?

I've already answered this question. The important dimension of marriage is its maturity and not its consummation. The marriage can be thoroughly consummated and still not represent the kind of mature, self-possessed, dedicated commitment that reflects the union between Jesus and the church. Note this fact well: sacrament means a creature or a relationship which tells us something about God, and a ceremony and a physical act do not by themselves even come remotely close to revealing the nature of God's love, unless and until the human love is sufficiently dedicated and sufficiently committed and that requires, as we have discovered with our new knowledge of human psychology, a good deal more maturity than we used to think. The point cannot be repeated too often—the Catholic change on the indissolubility of marriage (and it is a change) is based on a more sophisticated understanding of the psychological maturity that is needed for permanent marital commitment.

Andrew M. Greeley

37. Why has Ecumenism failed?

I don't think Ecumenism has failed at all. On the contrary, I think it has been an enormous success. In the space of a relatively few decades the Reformation and the Counter-Reformation had been brought to an end, and Catholics, Protestants, Jews and others are now talking to one another like friends, brothers and sisters, men and women of good will (except perhaps in Northern Ireland). This is fantastic progress and we should rejoice in it. If you mean by "failure" the fact that ecumenism has not eliminated denominational differences or has not yet produced a "super church," then a couple of points might be made.

1) There are still doctrinal and cultural differences among the denominations. Doctrinal differences could take a long time to work out even though considerable progress has been made in ecumenical conversations at the theological level. There was perhaps an unrealistic expectation in the years immediately after the Vatican Council that all these differences would go away. It has been relatively easy for Catholics and Anglicans and Orthodox, and even Lutherans, for example, to achieve broad doctrinal consensus. For Baptists and Fundamentalists, there is a long, long way to go and the discussions have only just begun.

2) It is not at all clear that the cultural differences ought to go away. One would hate, for example, to see the strong, vigorous piety of the Lutheran Church of Missouri Synod or the marvelous gospel music of the Baptist Church be blunted and absorbed out of existence. It may be that the proper model for ecumenism is not a super church but rather loose denominational cooperation in which the denominations come closer together in doctrine and in practice and in friendship and still maintain their authentic cultural and historical differences. The super church endeavors in the past have almost always failed and indeed ended up producing more, rather than fewer, denominations.

3) The Roman Curia does not want a church unit of any sort. It's recent torpedoing of the results of many years of work in the Roman Catholic Anglican dialogue indicates that the Curia does not want any other denomination hanging around Rome threatening its own power. There are very, very few differences (women's ordination being one of them) that prevent formal unity between Canterbury and Rome. But an Anglican presence within the broad Catholic community would be an enormous threat to the monopoly on power that the Roman Curias holds and the curial bureaucrats are simply not about to give that power up.

Despite these factors, however, the peace and the friendship and the cooperation among various denominations is a wonderful development. It happened more quickly than anyone would have thought possible and hence there is now some breathing space before we move on to the next phase, a phase whose precise direction is not yet clear. But the pause comes not from failure but from tremendous success.

38. Why can't Catholics practice birth control?

Well, in fact, most of them do, not only in the United States but in most of the other Catholic countries of the North Atlantic world, and they practice birth control because they are convinced that the Pope is simply wrong on this issue and that he and other church leaders do not appreciate how important sex is for keeping married love alive. Those who study the nature of human nature in the physical and biological sciences would agree that sex as a pair-bonding mechanism is more important in humans than it is in the rest of the primate species. Relatively frequent marital sex seems to be an essential part of human nature and when the church seems to want to inhibit and perhaps even prohibit this relationship, it is in the awkward position of seeming to violate one aspect of the natural law in the name of supporting another aspect.

Basically, the argument of the birth control encyclical is twofold:

a) The natural law is violated when some "artificial" impediment is used to prevent each and every act of marital intercourse from being open to the possibility of conception.

b) The sacramental symbolism of married love is violated when an impediment of an artificial nature is permitted to interfere with fertility.

This is the official, though non-infallible, teaching of the church. Many Catholic theologians and priests believe that the teaching can be reconsidered, especially because both the arguments seem dubious. Everything we know from the natural sciences about human nature suggests that that which is specifically human about the sexuality of our primate species is oriented towards pair-bonding and as long as the act of sexual intercourse is open to the possibility of pair-bonding it does not violate the essence of human nature. The overwhelming majority of Pope John's Birth Control Commission agreed with this position and argued that a marriage considered as a whole had to be open to the possibility of conception, but not necessarily each marriage act. Moreover, it is the almost unanimous experience of married couples that contraceptive intercourse does not interfere with the full expression of married love and does not lead to deterioration of respect for woman as church teachers insist that it does.

This controversy is one of the most serious that Catholicism has ever faced, both because of the great importance of sex in the lives of married people and because of the fundamental and pervasive dissent from the official teaching on the part not only of the married laity but also on the part of the lower clergy.

The root of the problem, it seems to me, is the absence of institutions of communication by which the laity can inform leadership of the church of the experience and wisdom of their married lives. The Pope, in his exhortation, *Familiaris Consortio*, has insisted that the married lay people have a unique and indispensible contribution to make to our church's understanding of marital morality by virtue of the charism of the sacrament of marital matrimony. Unfortunately, the birth control discussion has gone on now for fifty years with no attempt made to give the laity a chance to speak to the church leadership about their experience of married love, and in particular about their experience that the church's attitude on birth control creates an enormous impediment to the expression of married love. We have, it is to be feared, replaced the irreplaceable and dispensed with the indispensable. Until institutions of communication are established whereby the church leadership can listen to the authentic voice of the laity (and not merely to the voice of those laity who are chosen beforehand because they will say exactly what the church leadership wants them to say), the terrible and rending birth control crisis will continue.

In many countries, of course, the solution that is reached is that confessors insist in theory on the official teaching, but in practice, as a concession to human weakness, tolerate contraceptive intercourse. However, such a "pastoral solution" (apparently perfectly acceptable to the Curia) offends those of us who are part of the Northern European heritage who do not want to be told that our marital love is somehow or other weak or imperfect.

One has to say that in the present situation of non-dialogue, non-discussion, and non-communication during which officials eagerly talk out of one side of their mouths to endorse the papal position and just as eagerly talk out of the other side of their mouths when dealing with the pastoral practice of the clergy, the crisis does not seem likely to be solved for a long, long time.

39. Why does God permit evil in the world?

There is no adequate answer to that question. On the other hand, if one argues from the existence of evil that there is no God, there is no graciousness, there is no plan or purpose in life, then one is faced with the other problem of why there is good in the world. Christianity does not purport to offer an answer to the problem of evil. It merely purports to give us reasons for living bravely in the face of evil as Jesus did and being confident that in the long run goodness will triumph over evil. That there is a war in heaven and a war in the individual personality between good and evil is an empirical fact which is surely beyond discussion. But any attempts to explain why it is so and to eliminate the mystery of evil simply are not going to be successful. We will only understand the mystery of evil (including such awesome mysteries as the holocaust and the potato famine) when we are able to see the history of the cosmos and the history of humankind from God's perspective.

Andrew M. Greeley

40. Why are some actions that were considered mortally sinful before the Council no longer considered so?

First of all, preconciliar Catholicism tended to multiply mortal sins recklessly and prodigiously in order to terrify Catholics into staying in line, believing, despite what Jesus said, that fear was a more important motivation than love. Indeed, in many of its aspects, preconciliar Catholicism was obsessed with mortal sin as though it were the only reality in the world that mattered.

Some of the things that were alleged to be mortal sins in fact apparently never were intended to be so considered, including the Sunday Mass obligation as it was established by the Lateran Council. Other obligations "under pain of mortal sin" were of the canonical variety, such as meatless Friday previously discussed, and such laws were simply abolished. The ease with which they were abolished, however, raises some questions as to whether they were really such great obligations to begin with. For yet other sins, there is a tendency, in pastoral practice at any rate, to say that they may objectively be "grave," but the circumstances of the action frequently mitigate the gravity of the sin. The notion that circumstance—the absence of sufficient reflection and full consent of the will in the old terminology—was acknowledged even in the preconciliar moral theology. But clergy and teachers were reluctant to explain this principle as fully as they might in order that people, being excused from crossing a minefield filled with mortal sins, might relax, not try hard enough, and enjoy sinning. It never occurred to us in those days that the minefield seemed so perilous that many people would give up trying to avoid sin because they were convinced it was impossible to stay out of the "state of mortal sin" and hence, fear of mortal sin, intended to promote virtue, in fact promoted a despair over the possibility of virtue and an end of serious effort for the virtuous life.

While there is always the possibility that we may now have leaned in the opposite direction and become too generous and too sympathetic and too understanding, it is still true that the forgiveness that Jesus offered to the woman taken in adultery—even before she asked for forgiveness or expressed her sorrow—is a far more appropriate behavior for the church than the construction of elaborate and tricky minefields in which there are so many mortal sins which are so easy to commit that virtue seems impossible and forgiveness useless.

41. Why doesn't God continue to reveal himself right up to and including our day?

But of course God does continue to reveal himself in our own day through the sun in the morning and the moon at night, through the silly smile on the face of a child, through the touch of a friendly hand, through reconciliation after a quarrel, through sexual love, through the coming and going of the seasons, through music and art and poetry and fiction and friendship, through flowers and trees and mountains and lakes and streams and oceans and thunderstorms sweeping down out of the hills of Lebanon (or anyplace else, but Lebanon is where they are mentioned in the Psalms), through the fierce winter winds and the gentle spring breeze. All is through his grace, as Karl Rahner has said, and "everything is sacramental" as Nathan Scott has said. "God is every Being that lurks among the beings, in the sun shining on a wall, and in a crack in the sidewalk," as poet Richard Groban has told us.

Now you are going to say that's merely "natural revelation" and what you want is "supernatural revelation." But it is the same God, you see, who reveals himself through both forms of revelation. Moreover, the distinction, while valid up to a point, may ultimately miss the point, for the revelation of God's love in Jesus merely confirmed and validated the fact that our wildest expectations drawn from our experiences of natural revelation are indeed true. If you want signs and wonders and miracles you should go back and read St. Mark's Gospel and find out that that's not what Jesus is all about and if you wanted to know definitely where there is love in the universe, you are not likely to get any better proofs of it than the loves in your own life, for these loves are how God reveals his/her love to you.

42. Why is the priesthood a permanent state?

The old answer used to be because in the sacrament of orders a permanent "character" is placed on the soul of the priest. Exactly how a character can be placed on the soul was something that preconciliar theology never bothered to explain.

In the years after the Council, however, I think a number of theologians went to the other extreme and argued, in effect, that the priesthood was only a transient state, a temporary deputation by the local community which loses its validity when the local community withdraws the deputation.

I do not want to engage in theological controversy which is beyond my competence, but I will say that the more recent minimalistic descriptions of the priesthood are sociological nonsense. Once a man is set aside for those things that pertain to God, that act of having been set aside is something which becomes a characteristic of his personality (and it was probably the recognition of this characteristic which led originally to the "character" theology). You can no more eliminate the fact that you were once deputed to mediate between God and humankind than you can obliterate the color of your eyes, the shape of your skull, or even your skin color and your sexuality. A priest is a priest is a priest is a priest in virtually every culture that humankind knows. It may be altogether possible and indeed even acceptable and virtuous for a man to exercise the function of presiding over the Eucharistic and the religious community only for a certain period in his life. But the fact that he once played that role can no more be eliminated from his biography than can the fact that a man was a general in the Air Force or an all-American fullback—and for those defenders of the old character theology who think that being an all-American fullback is an "accidental" phenomenon, one simply has to say that they don't read the sports pages or watch television or understand what it means to be, let us say, a Heisman trophy winner.

In other words, the priesthood is a permanent state for the same reason that being a Heisman trophy winner is a permanent state—it's something that when it happens to you it's so important, it's always part of you for the rest of your life, no matter what else you may do.

43. Why do we try to prolong this life if happiness in the next life is the whole point of this life?

First of all, happiness in the next life is not the whole point of this life. The point of this life is to respond to the love that God offers us and to reflect that through the way we live, to bring more dignity and justice and charity and kindness and goodness into a world that desperately needs those things. This life is not a shell game, not a shadow existence, not a test to be passed like the college boards which we have to get by in order to make it into college. This life has a value, a dignity, and a worth of its own, and any attempt to minimize that is utterly foreign to the Catholic tradition, to the Scriptures and to the preaching of Jesus.

It is true, of course, that this life is a life of preparation, but we prepare by living this life to the fullest, by responding to its challenges to the best of our ability, and in a certain sense by acting in such a way that if there is not a life to come which continues this life, then the universe would be monumentally unjust.

On the other hand, one must also say that certain kinds of medical practice may very well prolong this life beyond what is appropriate, that we may keep people alive who for all practical purposes are no longer alive. The issue of when the life support system may be turned off, whether it should be turned off, and when it must be left on is complex. I don't think the moral theologians have caught up with it, but at least the theoretical principle is clear: We Catholic Christians believe that we should live this life to the fullest but we do not cling to it needlessly or beyond due course or in inappropriate ways because we believe that there is more wonder and surprise waiting for us in That Which Is To Come.

44. Why is the church so insistent on some elements of Christ's teaching but seemingly ignores or at least de-emphasizes others?

I'm not sure which teachings you think have been de-emphasized and which teachings emphasized, though I'll certainly agree that in recent years the church has been obsessed with problems of sexual ethics almost to the exclusion of everything else, and that more recently, some churchmen have become so obsessed with what they consider to be issues of peace and justice (issues in which they usually reflect the liberal/Marxist party line) that they, too, seem unaware that the Gospel is about God's love, his grace, his mercy, and his infinite capacity to surprise us with his astonishing and passionate affection for us.

But what can you do? Once there was a time when the Sorrowful Mother Novena was the big thing and another time when the Fatima devotion was the big thing and yet another time the lay apostolate. Now it is sex on the one hand, and peace and justice on the other—normally sex utterly misunderstood by the people who don't have wives and families of their own, who pontificate about it, and also peace and justice utterly misunderstood by men who think that enthusiasm and a few Marxist cliches are a substitute for economic and social competence. Jesus never guaranteed that the leaders and the teachers in his church would not include fanatics, ideologues, incompetents and dolts.

Andrew M. Greeley

45. Why is the church so ineffectual in Latin America?

There are a number of answers to that question, most of which have to do with an apparently incurable propensity of the clergy in the Hispanic tradition to identify religion with politics. The early missionaries were agents of Spanish imperialism. They equated the spread of the church with the spread of the Spanish empire and indeed seemed utterly incapable of self-criticism on this subject. With an astonishing and dogged persistence, the church continued to identify with conservative, aristocratic and oppressive regimes through most of the history of Latin America. When the so-called liberals came (mostly bourgeois "new class" who simply wanted to replace the old aristocracy as the power elite) they considered the church their natural enemy and did their best to get rid of clergy, particularly foreign missionaries. The result was that the church was identified with conservative and oppressive elements and lacked the resources in money and personnel to effectively educate the people. A decision was made early on, you see, that by controlling the political system and more-or-less forcing everyone to be Catholic, you didn't have to bother to educate them.

In fact, then, despite widespread folk piety and popular devotion, the church has never been institutionally very important to ordinary Latin

American Catholics and indeed has often been seen
as an enemy of the poor, the oppressed, the intellectual, and the upwardly mobile. The church is
ineffectual in Latin America because it has no
clout; that is to say, no capacity to influence the
attitudes and behaviors of its ordinary adherents
(most of whose adherence is tenuous and problematic and often mixed with pagan superstition).

There is no real evidence that the political
strategy has been recognized as ineffectual and
definitively rejected. Conservative church leaders
still ally themselves with military government, and
more radical and "revolutionary" clergy still identify with left-wing governments which, when they
obtain power, as in countries like Nicaragua or
Cuba, become every bit as oppressive and incompetent as their predecessors (Cuba and Cambodia, for
example, are the only two countries in the modern
world whose per capita income has declined in the
last twenty years). Whether they be on the left or
the right, Latin American Catholics tend to identify
politics with religion and to think that if you control the political system, you effectively preach
religion to the ordinary people and educate them in
the truths of the Christian faith.

Succinctly, the church is ineffectual in Latin
America because from the beginning, it had made a
monumental blunder and continues to repeat that
blunder.

46. Why have missionaries become more social than spiritual activists?

Perhaps the most important explanation is that the missionary vocation has undergone an enormous crisis since the Second Vatican Council and the recognition that the so-called pagan religions had values of their own which ought to be respected and honored. Unfortunately, the crisis in the missionary vocation did not lead to profound reconsiderations of what it means to be a missionary, but rather to the merging of facts, usually mixing vulgar Marxist ideology with pious words about "evangelization." In addition, many missionaries went through personal crises of faith in which they took the route of social activism as a substitute for religious conviction.

Finally, of course, there are many political and social injustices in missionary countries which ought to be corrected and which anyone with a Christian vision must be concerned about, although it is not clear that the Marxist ideologies which underpin so much of missionary activism would, in fact, do anything in the missionary country but make a bad social situation worse.

Many missionaries feel guilty, not without some reason, that in the past their religious communities were the agents, however unintentional, of Western cultural, if not political, imperialism; that, for example, they tried to impose on, let us say Korean society, a parochial model that might be more appropriate for Brooklyn or New York or Boston and tried to make the natives not merely Christians but also Westerners.

When all this is said, however, many of the old missionaries did remarkable work and Boston, Brooklyn and New York parishes often provided education, health, dignity for women, and many other good things that the societies otherwise would have lacked—on the whole, perhaps, more social improvement than the current political activist style of many missionaries might achieve. American missionaries, like most other American clerics and religions, were caught up in a post-conciliar crisis for which they were not prepared: the lack of depth of the training, of scholarship and of leadership, which would have enabled them in the transition crisis, to have coped without panic and without throwing out the baby with the bath water. It ought to have been possible to make nuanced changes in the missionary vocation, keeping all that was good from the past approach and adding new dimensions to it. Obviously, some missionaries have made such changes and have integrated the best of the old and the new. But all too many seem to have concluded that preaching Marx is an adequate substitute for preaching Jesus.

47. Why doesn't baptism make us all priests?

Well, it does, you know. We are all ordained by baptism to participate in the Eucharistic community when it comes together to eat the common meal. Just as any community can have only one chairman, the Eucharistic community has only one president, the ordained priest, but it is important to note that just as the community cannot come into existence (ordinarily) unless the president convenes, so neither can the president preside over the Eucharistic liturgy unless the community has been convened. (Perhaps for devotional purposes, priests can still say solitary masses, but in fact such masses do considerable violence to the community symbolism of the Eucharist.) Not everybody is an ordained priest because not everybody is the leader and the president of the Eucharistic community, but everyone is a priest in the sense that everyone is called to participate in that community.

48. Why does the papacy have so little influence in "Catholic Italy," which legally condones both divorce and abortion?

Whoever said Italy was Catholic?

Does a country become Catholic simply because the majority of its people are baptized Catholic and are rather innocent of any kind of Catholic education or spiritual formation?

Morever, the church in Italy still suffers (and will suffer for a long time to come) from the after-effects of the fact that the Pope was for many centuries the temporal ruler—an autocratic and dictatorial one at that—of a substantial segment of central Italy. The Pope, as a temporal ruler, seemed to many Italians the implacable enemy of the development of a democratic and unified Italy and, indeed, to many Romans, as the absolute enemy of self-goverance in the city of Rome itself. Memories of these conflicts die slowly. In the walls around the Vatican within the last century, were scenes of bloodshed as young Romans fought for the right of the people of the city to participate in their own government. Small wonder, then, that there is anti-clericalism, sometimes virulent, in the city of Rome (anti-clericalism which is, from the Italian viewpoint, utterly consistent with shouting enthusiasm for the bishop of Rome in the Piazza of St. Peter's). Quite simply, for many well-educated and liberal Italians, the church traditionally and historically has been the enemy, and even today often seems to be on the side of reactionary and sometimes corrupt powers in Italian political life. Neither is the papacy able to resist the temptation to intervene in Italian political issues. As sure as the Pope attempts to intervene in an issue facing the Italian electorate, a very considerable number of Italians will vote the other way to tell the Pope to keep his nose out of partisan Italian politics.

I would admit that it is a gosh-awful mess, but it is a mess that cannot be understood unless one realizes that as temporal rulers of the papal state, the popes were generally high-handed, authoritarian and oppressive and the Italian people have not forgiven the papacy for that historical fact (nor is it clear that the papacy and the curia realize the loss of the papal state was one of the best things that ever happened to the papacy).

49. Why can priests be dispensed from their priestly vows but laity not be dispensed from marriage vows?

At one level, this is a good question because a promise is a promise and a commitment is a commitment. Pope John Paul tightened up considerably on the dispensation of priests from their vows in order that it would be about as difficult for a priest to obtain a dispensation as it would for a lay person to obtain an annulment. And indeed most lay people who are incensed by the stern rules that now exist for priestly dispensation tend to change their minds when you point out that until recently it was much easier to be dispensed from your priestly vows than to be dispensed from your marriage vows.

However, there is a difference between the two sacraments. The union between man and woman is a union of person to person and when one breaks that union, one does tremendous harm to the other person. Moreover, it is also a union which is programmed genetically—and apparently reinforced by powerful hormone patterns—whereas the priestly commitment is not to another human person and the harm done to the community a priest serves by his departure is substantially less than the harm done to a spouse when a husband and wife depart. Moreover, there is certainly no biological or genetic or hormonal dynamism at work in the commitment that a priest makes. Quite simply, a marriage commitment is infinitely more important because of its natural and personalistic implications than is a priestly commitment, and the comparison between the two is invidious and misleading and ought to be abandoned.

50. Why are evil thoughts sinful if they do not lead to evil actions?

I'm not sure what you mean by evil thoughts but they are really only sinful in so far as they dispose to evil actions. Probably you mean "dirty" thoughts, the kinds of fantasies and desires and longings of the sort which are necessary to keep the human race going. One can eliminate sexual fantasies and desires from one's life only by ending the life or by eliminating all hormones from one's bloodstream. A desire for sexual intercourse with an appealing member of the opposite sex is about as natural as breathing and there is nothing necessarily "dirty" about such a reaction. On the other hand, when such fantasies are indulged in and become preoccupying and obsessive, they increase the likelihood that the other person is going to be "objectified," treated in the imagination as a thing instead of a person, and perhaps also treated in the real world like a thing instead of a person. A recent survey suggested that perhaps as many as a quarter of the men in the country would commit rape if they thought they could get away with it (and the proportion might be even higher if everyone was telling the truth). It ought to be pretty clear that such evil thoughts make life very dangerous for other human beings and that sexual fantasies need to be kept under careful control if they are not going to rather quickly cause us to do harm to others.

51. Why do so many Catholics feel that confession is no longer necessary?

It is certainly true many Catholics don't go to confession as often as they used to. Just the other day I checked some tabulations on the frequency of confession for a priest who was writing a dissertation about the art of being a good confessor. In the first ten years after the Vatican Council, the proportion of Catholics going to confession every month declined from 38% to 17% and almost half of young Catholics at the present time never go to confession (the proportion is a little lower in Canada where only 40 percent never go to confession). However, the discipline of the sacrament of penance (or reconciliation, as it is now called) has varied greatly in the course of Catholic history. In some monasteries, people went to confession several times a day. Some of the recent popes have gone to confession daily. On the other hand, in earlier eras of Christian history, people went to confession twice in their life: once when they went through a "conversion" experience, and the next time on their death bed.

I suspect there are many reasons for the decline in the frequency of the reception of Christian reconciliation. Catholics now take seriously what we always used to tell them, that it was not necessary to go to confession every time they received Holy Communion, and that there are many other ways for venial sins to be forgiven. Since Catholics are also less likely to see their lives strewn with mortal sin, they may feel they have less to confess. Furthermore, priests, perhaps feeling guilty about the mockery of the sacrament involved in some of the "automatic" confessions of the Thursday before First Friday, are much less likely to press people to go to confession. Finally, the cold, mechanical, impersonal and frightening style of confession in years gone by—with its propensity to scrupulosity, fears of bad confession, sacrilege, etc., etc., etc., turned off many laity and once they found that it was possible to be a good Catholic and ignore such horrendous experiences, they did so enthusiastically.

Like so many other things that have happened in the postconciliar era, an old, battered, inadequate and ultimately oppressive theory was swept away and nothing new replaced it. On the other hand, in those parishes where there has been careful instruction about the meaning of the sacrament of Christian reconciliation, it is certainly true that, while confessions are much less frequent, they are much better—more human, more devout, more reconciled and more edifying, both for priests and confessors.

I personally suspect that confession will be like the Gregorian Chant. It may take us twenty more years to rediscover what an excellent idea it is.

52. Why is the church opposed to homosexuality if the primary end of intercourse is no longer procreation?

I'll leave aside the question of what the primary end of intercourse is. Indeed, I am not sure that talking about the primary end is a very useful way to approach questions of human sexuality.

As for homosexuality, as I understand it, even the Vatican, while condemning it in theory, urges confessors to be tolerant, sympathetic and helpful in pastoral practice. One hears it said, for example, that seminary teachers even in Rome will say that, pastorally, a priest should try to persuade a homosexual to have stable rather than promiscuous relationships.

I simply don't know enough about the biology or the psychology of the matter to go beyond the previous statement. It may be that homosexuality is a result of genetic programming, or it may be the result of psychological experiences or it may be a combination of both. It may be that in some instances it is "curable" and it may be that in most instances it is not "curable." Homosexuals ought to be treated with respect and love, they ought not to be the objects of ridicule or discrimination. I would be very wary of saying that any given homosexual is committing a sin—but then I would be very wary of saying that any given heterosexual is committing a sin either, because the Scriptures tell me not to judge lest I be judged.

However, I am not prepared to say that "gay is good" in the sense that there is no real difference between heterosexuality and homosexuality. I don't think that's true and I don't believe there is any need to pretend that it is in order to support fairness and justice for homosexuals.

53. Why has the church of Christ become a big business?

It really isn't big business, you know. The Vatican's endowment is less than that of a small American liberal arts college and the annual budget, even in the largest archdiocese, is much less than the daily budget of most government agencies. Unfortunately, for those who complain about the church's financial concerns, there are no free lunches and if you want heat and light in your churches and schools, education for your children, care for the poor and the disadvantaged, alternative schools for inner-city Blacks, marital counseling programs, seminaries to educate priests, etc., etc., etc., it is going to cost money for those things and money must be collected, administered, sometimes invested and paid out. If you think that's "big business," then you don't know what you're talking about.

As a matter of fact, compared to the per capita budgets of other churches, American Catholics receive an enormous bargain. Catholic schools, for example, cost about one-half as much per student as do public schools and produce a much better quality of education. Some of this bargain basement cost for Catholic services is the result of low or non-existent overhead charges, but some of it, alas, is the result of the church's persistent refusal to pay living wages to its employees, including its priests and nuns. One might much more legitimately complain about that than one might complain about the church being big business.

There are two legitimate complaints Catholics might make about church financial activity. First of all, the fund-raising is often woefully inept. Catholics are not nearly as generous as their Jewish or Protestant counterparts, not because Catholics are inherently any less charitable but because the church is still following the fund-raising practices appropriate for an immigrant era. Moreover, Catholics might also complain about the incompetence and corruption which sometimes (rarely, perhaps, but still far too often) affects Catholic administration. In the absence of public accountability for the use of church funds, it is often a source of irresistible temptation, even for men who wear the sacred purple or the sacred crimson. The best book ever done on Catholic finances—James Gollin's *Worldly Goods*—began as an attempt to reveal the enormous financial wealth of the Catholic Church and concluded with the undramatic but accurate observation that the church is not wealthy, indeed not nearly as wealthy as it thinks it is, and that the real problem in the church is not excessive wealth, but inept fund-raising and administration (to which Mr. Gollin might add, if he were writing today, the occasional case of disgraceful corruption which hurts the image of even the most honest and responsible church administrators).

54. Why is there no effective religious education for Catholic youth outside of parochial schools?

I don't know what you mean by "effective." If you mean, why can't CCD programs do as well as Catholic schools, the answer is that it is naive to expect that you can accomplish in one hour a week something that is as effective as you can accomplish in twenty-five hours a week. Moreover, even though considerable resources have been put into CCD in the last twenty years, the rigid, Messianic ideology and general incompetence of those who administer CCD programs is in part responsible for their failure. Many, if not most, CCD administrators and directors view themselves as presiding over a social movement which is beyond criticism and beyond appraisal. CCD people have repeatedly tried to prevent the publication of research findings which show that Catholic schools are effective and that CCD is not and I have often been urged by CCD directors not to publish findings which will help "them," meaning Catholic schools.

Moreover, one cannot force young people to come to religious education programs in which neither they nor their parents are interested. Our evidence shows that about half the Catholics of high school age receive some kind of religious education—one quarter in Catholic schools and a quarter in CCD. The other half do not participate in programs either because they are not interested in religion or because their friends don't attend such programs or because their parents don't insist that they participate. How can the church be held responsible for that kind of indifference?

55. Why do we make so much of singing in the church when there is no mention in the Scriptures of Christ or his disciples singing?

Reread the Scriptures. After the Last Supper it is said that Jesus and his disciples sang a hymn before they went out to the Mount of Olives and St. Paul tells readers of one of his epistles that they should encourage one another with songs, psalms and spiritual hymns. Men and women sing to express their joy, their community, their love for one another. Singing is a natural, spontaneous and powerful form of human behavior. Religion without song is rare and nonexistent in the human condition. The practice of Catholicism for the last couple of hundred years in which there was no singing was perverse and inappropriate. If you don't like to sing in church, that's a reflection on you and not on singing.

On the other hand, it must be admitted that much of what passes for church music in contemporary Catholicism, is at very best, mediocre; church singing will only be adequate when we are willing to pay musicians and composers adequate incomes for their work. Moreover, parish singing is bound to be inept unless the pastor and his people in the parish council think that song worship of God is important enough to pay a decent salary to the men and women who are responsible for song worship in the parish.

It also must be acknowledged that unfortunately much of what passes for new church music is discouragingly banal. The church was once the most important patron of musical composition—it now patronizes trash. From Palestrina to the St. Louis Jesuits is a long way—all of it downhill.

56. Why do former priests want it both ways: to be relieved of their vows but still serve as priests?

First of all, as I said in my response to a previous question, more than half of them do not want to be priests at all and half of the remaining half only want to do occasional priestly work. The others really want to withdraw from the burdens of the commitment and still enjoy the advantages that come from it. They are all, of course, in favor of the abolition of the celibacy requirement, a move which would completely legitimate what they have done. I'm sorry, but I believe a commitment is a commitment and one ought to do everything in one's power to honor the commitment. If, for one reason or another, a commitment has to be revoked, it certainly doesn't seem appropriate to want to continue to enjoy the privileges along with the commitment. To use the marriage analogy, which as I noted before, is by no means a perfect one, it is as though some former priests are like married men who, having divorced their wives, perhaps even with an annulment, still want to sleep with them.

57. Why have the conciliar reforms resulted in a sharply declining church membership rather than the hoped-for resurgence?

I realize that this question is a cliche with the kind of Catholic liberals who enjoy reading *Commonweal*, but the assumptions simply are not true. There has not been a sharp decline in church membership. There has been some decrease in mass attendance but there has also been a doubling of the weekly rates of Communion reception (from 12 percent to 25 percent). When this figure is cited, the *Commonweal* liberal tends to poo-poo it, saying that the increase in Communion reception does not represent an increase in devotion, though how anyone can know that escapes me. Moreover, the decline in church attendance seems in substantial part to be a result of a life cycle phenomenon. Young people after college and before family formation tend to drift away from all major institutions, not merely the church. By the time they're in their early forties, however, they are as likely to be attending church as their parents.

Moreover, all the evidence in our research indicates there was a sharp upsurge in religious devotion in the years immediately after the Council and most of this was cancelled out by the negative impact of the birth control encyclical. Whatever one may say about the doctrinal validity of the encyclical (and one must not make judgments about such matters by taking surveys), one none-theless has to say that it had a powerful negative effect on Catholic devotion.

Finally, it is naive to the point of the imbecilic to expect instantaneous positive effects from an Ecumenical Council. It may be decades, even centuries, before the full effects of Vatican II are realized. Our own research evidence, for example, indicates that the young people born since the end of Council have a much different and much more positive religious sensibility than those who are only a few years older than they are. If one is to judge by such young people, the Council was an enormous success.

58. Why is the church doing so little about world poverty?

To begin with, you always speak of the church as though it's something distinct from yourself. You buy the pre-Vatican notions—false to the tradition—that the church is the bishops and the priests and the hierarchy, when in fact everybody is the church. You might legitimately rephrase the question to ask what you're doing about world poverty.

Moreover, what do you expect the church to do about the corrupt incompetency of the Mexican economy which is responsible for the fact that the country's great oil wealth hasn't filtered down to the ordinary people and that indeed the foul-up there is now so great that the Mexican economy is in worse shape than it ever was? What do you expect the church to do about Venezuela where all the wealth has gone to the building of soccer stadiums, expressways and high-rise apartment buildings (and this in a country where there are free and democratic elections)? What can the church do about socialist Cuba whose administrative incompetence has virtually destroyed that country's agricultural economy? What is the church to do about countries like Pakistan and Bangladesh where it has no influence at all? How is it to deal with the horrendous foul-up of the free distribution system in Central Africa, or the rigid control of prices in many African agricultural countries which makes it impossible for farmers to effectively do business?

I remember when my friend, Pat Moynihan, was Ambassador to India and the United States was still keeping India alive by enormous grain shipments. Pat remarked to me one day in New Delhi, "There has to be something, something that will work here that will help them to solve their food problem."

There was indeed something and the administration which succeeded Ms. Gandhi, however incompetent it may have been in many respects, did solve India's food production problems with a single action. The anti-Gandhi party was largely based on peasant movements and virtually its first action upon taking office was to remove government restrictions on agricultural prices, thus giving Indian farmers much more motivation to increase their production. Now India is self-sufficient in food and indeed is able to export food to other countries. What do you expect the church to do about that?

Back in the middle and late 70's, when it was liberal faddism to proclaim a world food shortage, groups like "Bread for the World" were ranting about the fact that Americans ate too much meat and the grain that was going to feed beef cattle could instead be sent to the poor countries, to be eaten or stored away in grain reserves against the famine that was certain to come. We were even urged, in some cases by people who knew better, to give up meat one day a week in order to make more grain available for the rest of the world. The American hierarchy, in one of the many foolish and ill-considered statements it made at the urging of its peace and justice staff, urged the establishment of a world grain reserve.

Now we hear nothing much about these sorts of policies as the world has a food glut at least as severe as the oil glut. Nor does anybody note that the ranting about famine or "Bread for the World" and other groups flew in the face of the expertise of the nation's best agricultural economists. Those who understand the economics of lesser developed nations—as opposed to those who pontificate about such subjects without understanding them—will tell you that the principal cause of world poverty is in the inequity of the distribution system within these countries, and that the transfer of funds from affluent to less affluent countries—unnecessary as it may be—would be an utter waste, unless and until the political, social and economic structures of such countries are transformed so that the money coming from the affluent countries would in fact go to poor people and not to government bureaucrats. How is the church supposed to accomplish such internal reform especially in countries which are not Catholic or in which Catholicism has little political influence? There are a lot of cliches kicking around among semi-educated clerics and religious who are messing in problems of justice. Of these, two of the worst are 1) that poor countries are poor because the rich countries are rich, and 2) the United States has only a small proportion of the world's population but it consumes an enormous proportion of the world's resources.

The first assertion is simply and utterly false, even though demagogues in the Third World countries, appealing to the envy of their people, insist on it, and a lot of demagogic clergy in those countries do too. It is not in the interest of the rich countries to keep poor countries poor. On the contrary, the affluent countries have every reason to want the poor countries to be affluent, too, so they can buy more of the goods produced in the rich country. The poverty of the poor countries is to a very great extent the result of internal structural deficiencies in the economy and the society of those countries, and the problems of poverty will not be solved by outside intervention unless there is also internal change. Moreover, the fact that the United States imports raw materials and exports manufactured goods is not called exploitation, it's called world trade, a phenomenon which left-wing Catholics seem to find oppressive. But consider what would happen if we stopped importing coffee from Latin American countries which produce coffee beans. The economy of those countries would collapse and many people in them would starve to death. Consider also the fact that the United States is one of the largest exporters of raw materials in the world and that indeed America's agriculture industry is its most successful exporting business and that American farmers feed half the world. Do the ranting and raving peace and justice folks want that stopped?

Andrew M. Greeley

59. Why is the church ignoring critical environmental problems?

What do you expect the church to do about pollution of the Caspian Sea in Russia? Or the Rhone River in France? The church can certainly insist on proper respect for physical creation and it seems to me that it has done so, but it has no competency to deal with some of the complex issues that are involved in environmental questions. And to expect the church to be competent, much less to back one side or the other in these intricate debates, is to expect the absurd and the impossible. As Robert Tucker has pointed out in his recent book on the environmental movement, a substantial component of environmentalism is elite snobbery in which the affluent, in the name of respect for physical creation, wish to deny affluence to those who are less affluent than they. The church ought to be just as critical of some of this environmental snobbery as it is of the various health problems of pollution. Nonetheless, it must also be realized that some environmental enthusiasts are utterly anti-technological and wish to turn the clock back to an earlier period. (I remember one experiment in England where a group of people lived for a year like their Bronze Age ancestors and celebrated the fact that they were able to survive very nicely. Of course, they continued to have all the appropriate innoculations for their children and the women continued to use their birth control pills, thus solving problems the Bronze Age people experienced in high birth rates and high infant mortality rates and negating the experiment entirely.) In the 19th century, Lake Michigan (to choose my favorite body of water for discussion) had a lot less environmental pollution than it does today—and it was teeming with cholera germs. While I want the lake to be cleaner, and it is cleaner than it was ten years ago, I still think the trade-off between technology and cholera germs is a good one.

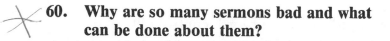

60. Why are so many sermons bad and what can be done about them?

Sermons are bad because priests are not trained to be preachers in the seminary, because they do not take their responsibility of preaching seriously, and because they do not prepare their sermons well. And they get away with this violation of justice—the laity have a right to hear the gospel preached well—because lay people let them get away with it.

The National Federation of Priests' Councils every year votes resolutions against virtually any injustice that may be thought to be existing in the world, but it never condems the injustice of a rotten Sunday homily.

Preaching preparation in the seminaries is abominable. It is thought much more important that seminarians acquire "clinical pastoral experience" or do "field service work" than that they learn how to read and write, to express themselves clearly and articulately and vigorously and imaginatively. Indeed, some young priests are convinced that all they need to be is spontaneous and "talk from the heart"—to such an extent that in principle they refuse to use the various homiletic newsletters that are available. In fact, preaching is a form of communication. It is an art and it is acquired by practice. It is an exercise of the imagination and the imagination is developed by experience in reading of imaginative works and writing imaginative works. If I had to choose for seminarians between clinical pastoral experience and reading Shakespeare, I would enthusiastically opt for the latter because reading Shakespeare would help them preach and preaching is, according to our empirical evidence, the single most important thing a priest does. Moreover, I don't think anybody should be ordained who hasn't written at least one novel, or twelve sonnets, or three or four short stories, and thus demonstrates that he has some capacity for imaginative expression. Religion, as our research at NORC has demonstrated, takes its power and its origin in the imagination and when religion and religious communication is deprived of imaginative content, it becomes pretty worthless. Yet most clergymen have atrophied imaginations because they do not think creative writing has anything to do with the ministry.

Finally, many if not most priests know they're bad preachers (80 pecent of the laity give us poor marks on sermons, so many of us are bad preachers), but they have despaired of improving the quality of their preaching and therefore they refuse to think about how bad they are and become highly incensed when someone like me repeatedly asserts that preaching is terrible (a sure way to get your column dropped from a Catholic newspaper is to write about preaching—and lay editors will almost certainly write an editorial condemning such a column, saying I have a one-track mind—even though if one mentions preaching in a talk with laity present, they want to talk about nothing else for the rest of the evening).

Because of their fear that they cannot improve themselves, the clergy bury their heads in the sand and pretend to themselves that the laity are not furious about the abominable state of preaching and the laity are still a little bit too embarrassed to tell Father what a mess he made of the Sunday homily.

If preaching is a skill, a craft, an art that can be acquired, even if in the acquisition one has to go through some wrenching personality changes which may involve short-term psychotherapy, priests' associations and priests' senates should take it as one of their highest priorities to set up comprehensive programs to improve the quality of preaching, and lay people might want to consider organized campaigns to withhold Sunday contributions unless preaching committees are set up in the parish to improve the quality of homilies.

Alas, I don't think either of these actions is going to be taken, so the homilies will continue to be rotten.

61. Why did the change to the vernacular result in declining Mass attendance?

It didn't result in declining Mass attendance. That's a typical *post hoc ergo propter hoc* argument. The overwhelming majority of American Catholics—87 percent—approve of the vernacular liturgy. Mass attendance declined, as I said before, for two reasons. First of all, because of the new life-cycle phenomenon which did not exist in years gone by in which young people are alienated from all organizations, and not merely the church, and secondly, because of the negative impact of the birth control encyclical. Admittedly, the vernacular liturgy is sometimes badly performed. When a priest mumbled the Mass in Latin, it did not bother anybody. When he mumbles and stumbles in English, it grates on the nerves of the laity. When the Epistle was read inarticulately in Latin, it didn't matter. Now that it is read inarticulately in English, it does matter, but people don't stop going to church for those reasons.

It is also the case that Catholics are now much more likely to accept excusing reasons for not going to Mass on Sunday than they used to. Few people still feel obliged to drag themselves to church if they have a 101° temperature, and so this more relaxed—and more sensible—attitude toward the Sunday obligation may also account for some of the declining Mass attendance. It is simply not right to attribute the decline in Mass attendance to the vernacular.

62. Why have so many of our young people lost interest in the church?

As I have said in response to several previous questions, there is now a life-cycle phenomenon in which young people in the post-college and pre-married years are alienated from all organizations including the church. This alienation tends to end as they become older and marry and have children. They tend to reaffiliate with various institutions—so that there is a correlation between the return of young Catholics to religious practice and to Democratic party affiliation.

Some of this alienation is the hold-over from the faddish, fashionable posturing of alienation that marked the young people of the late sixties and early seventies. The evidence in our research on those who are presently teenagers suggests that this fashion is changing, though gradually, and that the alienation of young people in the decade ahead will be less than it was in the decade behind.

However, the church itself is by no means free from blame for the problems. We have gone through a sustained period in which clergy simply were not interested in working with young people and dismissed work with young people as part of the "kiddy" apostolate, and many parish priests think they are too busy to be bothered with young people. A substantial number of Catholic parishes in the country have no young adult or teenage programs and many of these are in cities in which there are heavy concentrations of young unmarrieds who are completely ignored by the church (at the same time that the peace and justice bureaucrats are pontificating about the Third World). Moreover, young people find little guidance from the clergy in their struggle for sexual maturation. Indeed, all they hear from the church is what often seems to them to be mindless repetition of prohibitions which are not justified by anything in the way of sensible or sensitive arguments, but merely by the old cliche that these things are wrong because the church says they are wrong and you've got to do what the church tells you to do.

In short, while there is an inevitable period of alienation in the young adult phase of the life-cycle (at the present but perhaps it will change), the church has so badly fouled up its ministry to young people that it seems to have driven many of them away—and in some instances one has the impression that churchmen are proud of having driven them away. Then when they begin to drift back, the church, with continued and stupid insensitivity, welcomes them back with "guidelines;" that is to say, an elaborate system of rules and obligations which make the old Canon Law seem liberal by comparison. To answer your question briefly, young people have lost interest in the church partly because of a life-cycle phenomenon and partly because of the arrogant stupidity of the clergy.

63. Why is the parochial school system being dismantled when it contributes so much to the church in America?

Because the bishops have been foolish, that's why.

And the worst of the foolishness are the attempts in many dioceses to dismantle Catholic school systems in the inner city which are serving minority groups, many of whom are not Catholic. This inner city educational ministry is the most impressive work and service in which the American Church has ever engaged, and while some archdioceses, like New York, have enthusiastically and imaginatively supported this inner city school apostolate, other dioceses have done their best to abandon it. It is interesting to note that during the entire seventeen years of Cardinal Cody's administration in Chicago, not a single parochial school classroom was opened (and hundreds were closed) in what was the largest Catholic school system in the world, and this despite the insistent demands of lay people for more Catholic schools.

While the clergy in theory still support Catholic schools, in practice it's a lot easier and a lot cheaper to settle for CCD. Building and maintaining Catholic schools requires effort and the CCD ideology has dispensed many suburban pastors from that effort. The only ones who really seem to want Catholic schools are parents and their vote doesn't have much clout in the Catholic Church as it is presently organized.

64. Why should we have permanent deacons when lay persons can indeed perform the same functions?

Well, I think there are some functions, officiating at marriage, for example, or even officially preaching on Sunday, that lay people can't perform. Nonetheless, with characteristic superficiality, American Catholicism rushed into a program of ordaining deacons without having any clear theoretical reason for doing so. Even in my own diocese, the rationale for deacons seemed absolutely the same as the rationale heard twenty years ago for a lay apostolate. I think it's a good idea to have permanent deacons for the church, but I don't think the priests are willing to accept them as full-fledged clergy (and of course they are full-fledged, they are in sacred orders), much less to give them serious and responsible positions. (And these problems are linked to the prior problem—nobody is quite sure what deacons are for. If one should suggest, for example, that the financial administration of the diocese ought to be in the hands of the deacons, most of the priests and bishops would be horrified, but in fact that is why the deaconate first came into existence and that's the role they played in the early church).

Andrew M. Greeley

65. Why have nuns deserted the educational apostolate?

I suspect that part of the identity crisis of religious orders of women in our day involves a questioning of everything the religious orders had been doing, and since most of the religious orders of women had been teaching in Catholic schools, it is inevitable that as women tried to find what had gone wrong with the religious life, they would blame the educational apostolate and seek almost any other kind of activity as more relevant and educational—which is to say, more emotionally satisfying and more responsive to the problems that beset them. In fact, the overwhelming empirical evidence suggests that the educational apostolate of the Catholic orders of women is the greatest contribution to social justice ever made in the American church. For several generations, the Catholic schools have facilitated the movement out of poverty of various ethnic immigrant groups, now most recently Black and Hispanic immigrants, and that the nuns who have taught in the Catholic schools have made greater contributions to peace and justice than anybody else in the church. It is dubious that any other of the apostolates in which sisters engage have had anywhere near as important an impact.

It does not follow, of course, that the only possible role for religious women is teaching school, and surely in this day and age religious women should have a good deal of freedom about what kind of apostolic activity is appropriate for them. But the choice of other kinds of work ought not to be made out of contempt for the educational apostolate or the conviction that the educational apostolate has "failed," or on the grounds that Catholic education is "irrelevant." Indeed, it is one of the most relevant activities in which the American church has ever engaged.

Andrew M. Greeley

66. Why are Marxist principles incorporated in Liberation Theology?

Mostly because liberation theologians are romantic fools.

They are motivated by a very proper concern for social injustice, for misery, poverty and suffering, and they also believe that it is the function of Christians committed to the message of Jesus to do all in their power to mitigate and even eventually eliminate such injustices—positions which are certainly unexceptionable. However, their conviction that Marxism is a solution to problems of social injustice and political oppression simply will not stand the test of an half-hour's reading of the daily newspapers. The Soviet Union is a corrupt, oppressive and inefficient society, so too is the Communist government in countries such as Poland, Romania and East Germany. Quasi-communist governments in Africa have utterly failed economically and in most cases have ruined the economies of potentially prosperous countries like Mozambique. The per capita income in Cuba has gone down under Communist rule. Mao's China was an economic failure and the new regime in China, in order to undo that failure, is turning more and more to the "capitalist line." One cannot think of a single instance anywhere in the world where a Communist government has been able to sustain prosperity for a long period of time, and certainly not a single instance of a Communist dominated government where there is freedom. In the face of this overwhelming evidence, the vulgar Marxism (meaning Marxism which rarely involves the reading of Marx himself) of the liberation theologian is stupidity of the highest order. Marxism has never eliminated social injustice, never solved economic problems, and never brought political freedom.

I've heard missionaries who are sympathetic with the Marxist position argue, "things are so bad in our country that nothing, not even Communism, could make them worse." Those who had to suffer under Communist rule might disagree, but Communism generally does make the lot of the people in the country worse. It also deprives them of what shreds of political freedom they might have had.

Most liberation theologians are innocent of any understanding of the complexities of sociology and economics. They know nothing about agricultural and industrial development. Moreover, because they are clergymen and theologians they claim a clerical discount which excuses them from understanding these subjects Therefore, a quote from Marx or from a Marxist philosopher or economist substitutes for empirical understanding of the complexities of problems in poor countries. To be a Marxist revolutionary sounds brave and heroic and impressive and generous, and for the romantic liberation theologian this is all that is required. It is not necessary that one be wise, sophisticated or even well-informed. You show your concern about poverty, in other words, by being a Marxist.

Furthermore, most intellectuals in under-developed countries, and indeed many European intellectuals, are convinced that Marxism is the wave of the future, that eventually Marxism will triumph all over the world and that therefore by becoming a Marxist one is not only radical and revolutionary and committed to the cause of social justice, but one is also riding the wave of history. This conviction about the eventual triumph of Marxism is of course utterly unconfirmed by the actual situation in Marxist countries, but that fact does not seem to disturb either the intellectuals or the liberation theologians who want to jump on the Marxist bandwagon.

Liberation theology as a concrete social, political and economic program does not even begin to exist. Indeed, as theology it is generally shallow, inferior and simplistic, but because it is "Third World" it is granted a discount by many Catholic theologians who ought to know better and who do not face up to and criticize its simplisms and absur-dities—a form of theological tokenism which is not fair to the Third World theologian but is really a not particularly subtle or sophisticated brand of tokenism.

67. Why do cults appeal to so many modern youth?

Well, cults appeal only to a relative minority of modern youth, and then for the most part, only for a brief period of time. Generally, young people to whom the cults appeal are those who come from families with very vague religious backgrounds in which there is almost no explicit religious training—Protestant and Jewish families which are in fact agnostic for all practical purposes. The young people turn to the cults because they are looking for something in which to believe and because their families did not provide them with something in which to believe. The cults also appeal to those personalities who need comprehensive disciplines and answers from authority figures, simple and easy answers for all the questions in life (the same kind of person who in the past perhaps was attracted to certain kinds of religious and monastic communities). Much of the appeal of the cults, in other words, is more the result of psychopathology than religion.

Andrew M. Greeley

68. Why has the position of priests as leaders in society sharply diminished?

I suppose the principal reason is that Catholics are no longer uneducated and unsophisticated immigrants who needed their priests to be not only religious leaders but political, social and economic leaders, too. It doesn't seem to me that the position of priests as religious leaders has diminished at all, save perhaps in the minds of many priests who think that the development of the lay apostolate and various lay ministers in parish life has reduced them to Mass-sayers and absolution-givers. In fact, in the minds of the laity priests are still the religious leaders par excellence and indeed perhaps more important than they've ever been before. Surely, in our research, the correlation between the quality of ministry of the parish priest and the religious behavior of Catholics is awesome.

Moreover, it would be, I think, something of a mistake to overestimate how much power priests had in the past. I suspect that often the immigrant pastors were not nearly as influential in the world beyond church life as history books and our selective memories might make us believe. *Some* immigrant pastors were indeed extraordinarily influential, but others may have had much less influence in their neighborhood or their own community than do some of our collegial, democratic, outgoing, post-conciliar pastors.

69. Why is the devil being down-played?

There is obviously evil in the world, evil that goes far beyond the malice of individual personalities, cosmic evil, a war in heaven in which good and evil struggle for possession of the universe and evil often seems to be winning. The devil was a useful myth or story for describing the undoubted phenomenon of the struggle between good and evil. The idea of the devil was taken over by Judaism and Christianity from the Persian religion in which the problem of evil was explained by a conflict between a good guy and an evil guy who were more or less equal in strength, though finally, at the end, the Persians fudged because when the last battle was over, the god of good triumphed, however narrowly, over the god of evil. In Judaism, however, even as late as the Book of Job, Satan was not an evil angel, but rather a member of God's court who was a bit of a trickster; that is to say, still a good angel.

Contemporary scripture studies call into question whether the scriptures really intend to say as a matter of objective fact that there are angels and devils who represent goodness and evil personified. The angels of Yahweh are considered, according to these scholars, merely to be manifestations of Yahweh's power and the devils merely to be the forces of evil that are working in the world. Be that as it may, one of the problems in the "Exorcist" approach to the devil is to reduce the forces of evil to a malign spirit that makes little girls say dirty words and vomit. Evil is far more serious than the devil in the "Exorcist" and infinitely more serious than Mephistopheles or even Bill Cosby playing Satan.

If there is a down-playing of the devil today, the reason is that emphasis on the personification of evil that leads us to minimize the human capacity for evil and to attribute to the devil the evils that are caused by sinful structures in the human condition would in fact weaken us in our struggle against evil. It does not mean necessarily that one concludes that evil is not personified; one rather concludes that concentrating on the personification of evil may interfere with the struggle against evil.

Incidentally, whatever the Scripture scholars say, I hope that there are angels and I'll be terribly disappointed if there are not.

70. Why doesn't the church encourage the mystical tradition?

Here we go again with "the church." I am sure you can find lots of Roman documents and papal speeches praising the mystical tradition and you can find a fair number of Catholics who read Teresa of Avila, John of the Cross, Juliana of Norwich, Walter Hilton and the author of *The Cloud of Unknowing,* and of course that wonderful English mystic whose book, *Fires of Love,* is available in the Penguin paperback, Richard Rolle.

Admittedly, in its classroom teaching and its Sunday preaching, American Catholicism seems unaware of the mystical tradition, even though the Paulist Press' mysticism series seems to have done quite well, and even though almost two-fifths of American Catholics have had at least one mystical experience.

I suppose there are two reasons why American Catholicism is not much interested in the mystical. We are, after all, a pragmatic church, barely out of the immigrant era, still interested in buildings, organizations, accomplishments and achievements. We do not have the serenity, the relaxation, the calm to pay much attention to mysticism. Moreover, many of our clergy are just a little bit suspicious of mystics. Are they not, after all, perhaps some kind of freaks who are engaged in self-deception? John of the Cross, Teresa of Avila, or Richard Rolle would not be all that welcome, I suspect, as members of a parish council or parish school board.

I remember once when I was at a meeting at which Charles Davis, the theologian, was also present. I mentioned in my presentation the possibility that Catholicism should be seriously concerned about rediscovering its mystical heritage. Davis asked me what I meant about the Church's mystical heritage, suggesting that perhaps there was no such thing.

I confess that I was a little frightened because I didn't know much about that heritage myself (I fear I am one of the least mystical of people) and was afraid that Davis had some profound objection which was going to make me feel and look very foolish. Gritting my teeth, I said something about John of the Cross, Teresa of Avila, Eckhart, Suso, Mechtilde, Magdeburg, and of course Richard Rolle, Walter Hilton and Juliana of Norwich.

"Oh, yes, quite, I see." said Davis.

I didn't and I still don't, but I suppose in an age of simplistic liberation theology and instant solutions to complex issues of peace and justice, nobody is much interested in mysticism.

71. Why are your answers to so many of these questions querulous?

Not because I am angry at the people who ask the questions, though there is a sort of stubborn refusal in many of these questions to give up old and discredited models of the church. I am rather angry at those teachers (teachers of mine included) who served up such an inadequate, limited, rigid, and 'nsensitive version of Catholicism which makes it possible and even necessary for people to still ask these questions.

72. Why remain a Catholic if church leaders and teachers can make such terrible mistakes?

Why not remain a Catholic? What are the alternatives? It may not be currently all that good a church, but it's the only one we have, and besides, however imperfect immigrant counter-reformation Catholicism may be, it is still my link with the Catholic past, it is still the place where I learned about God and Jesus and Mary and the Christian traditions, my heritage, my tradition, my church. For all its faults, I love it, and I have no intention of leaving it behind.

73. **Why should the rest of us stay in the church when it is so filled with imperfection?**

Look, find a perfect church and then join it, only realize the day that you join it, it will stop being perfect.

74. Why does the church still distinguish between priests and laity?

It still distinguishes between priests and laity because priests and laity have different roles and different functions in the church. From the very beginning of Christianity, certain men have been set aside to preside over the Eucharistic Assembly and to act as religious leaders of the community (my hunch is that at certain times in history women did this too, but that there has been a monumental coverup to hide this historical fact). There continues to be both a theological and sociological need today for religious leadership. It is impossible to imagine any kind of religious communities that would not have certain official leaders, and while certain minimalist theologians would try to argue that there is no solid historical or theological reason for there to be priests distinct from the laity, these writers tend to ignore the overwhelming sociological need for religious leadership in every community that humankind has ever known.

To say that priests and lay people have different roles and functions is not to say the clergy IS the church or that clerical monopoly on power is justified or that the clericalist mentality and style of the past couple of centuries ought to continue or that the clergy have a right to lay down rules and regulations which the laity must follow (be they on social action or sexual morality or six month marriage preparations). It is also true that many of those who are quickest to criticize the clericalism of the Right have no problem with the clericalism of the Left—i.e., the intervention of the clergy to support left-wing political causes or policies. Thus, liberation theology in Latin America has always seemed to me to be one more dubious continuation of the clericalism of the Spanish Empire. Having supported right-wing political regimes for centuries, the church is now trying to support left-wing political regimes, as though the clerical office gives men the power and competence to make political decisions and to take political steps which are binding on the laity.

Our own research evidence, in fact, shows that priests may be more important as religious leaders in American Catholicism than ever before, despite the fact that many priests want to run as far as they can from the responsibility of being a religious leader. Neither those who wish to minimize the importance of theological and religious functions of the clergy or wish to convert these functions to one of social action leadership have the slightest understanding of the needs of ordinary people or the inevitabilities of the sociology of religion.

Andrew M. Greeley

75. Why was Canon Law revised and what does it mean?

My opinion is that revision of Canon Law is much ado about nothing. The average Catholic lay person, and even the average parish priest, could not care less about the code of Canon Law. The revision does not notably change the canonical mentality as such in the church, or the perspective of men such as the late Cardinal Pericle Felici who argued with considerable conviction that people existed for laws instead of vice versa. Canon Law is only important if you reduce the church to a system of laws, something to which we came awfully close to doing in the religion classes of the pre-Vatican Council church, something which all too many Catholics still believe today.

The church probably needs some kind of constitution and by-laws like any human organization; it does not, however, need more than seventeen hundred rules. A statement of a hundred or so basic principles of church organization would have been useful. The present slight revision of the Code is of little use and of little interest and of little importance. It may be that women are no longer equated with morons and children as they were in the old Code, but they still are not given full rights. Admittedly, psychological immaturity is now written into the Code as one of the grounds for annulment of marriage, but the new review added to the annulment process will simply make it longer and more tedious and more oppressive. The Code of Canon Law does not provide for members of the church what every constitution has provided since 1789—an authentic Bill of Rights and the guarantee of due process of the law. The church vigorously demands such rights from other institutions but it is apparently not itself willing to concede such rights to its own members.

The less said, then, about the new code of Canon Law, the better—and the sooner it's forgotten, the better.

76. Why are some dioceses making the process of conversion more difficult by insisting on the so-called "Rite of Christian Initiation for Adults?"

Apriorism, legalism, and clericalism did not die with the Second Vatican Council. The so-called RCIA is an aprioristic, theoretical, clericalist effort to reassert control over lay people. It is an attempt to mold converts, not into the kind of Catholic the Holy Spirit inspires them to be, but the kind of neo-clericalist Catholic that liturgical historians with no flexibility, no sociological knowledge, and no sensitivity to the modern world want them to be.

The argument that the RCIA is a new "catechumenate" would be more convincing if it demonstrated the slightest sensitivity to human needs, aspirations and learning behavior. As it is, the RCIA is one more example of the dreadful pall of historical apriorism, of lifeless and superficial scholarship which some liturgists are trying to impose on the church. Hopefully, the cult of the RCIA will simply be one more gimmicky fashion that will go down the same pike in which previous fads such as "Salvation History" disappeared during the last two decades. As it is, men and women have the right to the sacrament. The current clericalist propensity to interfere with the exercise of that right by insisting on so-called "guidelines" which are in fact, enormously burdensome rules, is a crime that calls to heaven for vengeance.

77. Why the wide disparity in diocesan policies regarding women's participation in the liturgy?

Look, you've got to get used to it: like I've said before, the church is a pluralistic institution. It manifests itself in different shapes, in different times and places. We've never been quite so uniform as we liked to think we were forty years ago, but if uniformity is something you need in your religion, then you really shouldn't bother with Catholicism. The differences which are to be found in many matters in different dioceses are largely the result of the personality and mentality of the Bishop and the traditions of the clergy and the people. In particular, with regard to women's rights and women's functions in the church, a good deal depends upon to what extent the Bishop is a male chauvinist on the one hand, and to what extent he's willing to risk the wrath of Rome by leaving the matter of women's participation to the discretion of his parish priests.

Andrew M. Greeley

78. Why the current de-emphasis on sin?

I'm not aware that the church has de-emphasized sin: we still don't like it. However, we're more aware now than we were in the past that Jesus did not come to preach about sin and that the essence of the Christian message does not deal with human sinfulness but with God's love. Even the empirical evidence shows that love of God rather than fear of God is much more likely to produce virtuous behavior. There was a time in the past when we became a totally sin-oriented religion. This approach was a perversion of the Gospel and, thank heaven has been abandoned at long last. There may well be some clergy and religious teachers who now pretend there is no such thing as sin at all. They have simply gone to the other extreme but my impression is that we have a long, long way to go to eliminate the pernicious notion that our faith is nothing more than a series of negative rules.

79. Why are there three readings at mass now?

Oh, lots of reasons. First of all, they give inarticulate and ill-trained readers a chance to affront and offend the congregation. They also provide an opportunity for prissy liturgical purists to spread a miasma of dullness and boredom over one more aspect of Catholic life. They provide an excuse for poor sermons because priests make fools of themselves for briefer periods of time. It is also necessary to have three readings because there is not enough material to preach on in just one reading and because, since neither literacy nor the printing press have been invented, how else are the Christian people to read the scriptures?

Andrew M. Greeley

80. Why do some priests still think masturbation is a mortal sin?

Perhaps because their "Supreme Sacred Congregation for the Defense of the Faith" insists that it is a serious sin. Many, if not most priests, however, take the "pastoral" view that while in theory masturbation may be gravely sinful, in practice, it often is not because of immaturity or the power of passion to deprive the person of full freedom.

Some scholars point out that it was not a sin over which there was much concern for more than 1500 years of Catholic history and that to the extent it was considered sinful, often the violation was against justice instead of against chastity because "wasting the seed" might interfere with the transmission of the family line and the family property. A full discussion of this῀ problem must necessarily await the development of solid historical, theological, cultural and sociological Catholic theory of sexuality which goes beyond the repetition of negative prohibition. The Pope's Wednesday Audience Talks provide a solid basis for the development of such a theory but few Catholic theorists seem ready to risk it yet.

81. Why is the church opposed to oral and anal sex?

It opposes such behavior on the grounds that they're "unnatural" acts though the "unnaturalness" of them is based in most Catholic theorizing on the fact that they are de facto, a form of contraception, sexual pleasure enjoyed in such a way as to interfere with the mechanics of procreation. If one believes, as many Catholic theorists and most Catholic laity do, that contraception is not necessarily always sinful, another argument must be found that these "perversions" are in fact unnatural and sinful. On the other hand, it is absurd to insist, as do some modern sex manuals, that oral sex in particular, is almost a matter of obligation.

As a general principle, husbands and wives should remember that affection should finally be judged by whether it intensifies the love of their marriage union.

Andrew M. Greeley

82. Why is the church still canonizing saints?

One of the worst things about the post-Vatican church is that we have given up on saints, angels, souls in purgatory, statues, stained glass windows and other wonderful elements of the Catholic heritage. So much of Catholic education in days gone by consisted of mothers telling their children stories about the saints, the angels, and the souls in purgatory. Unfortunately, an oppressive hyper-literalism has deprived us of many of these story-telling resources, just as a hyper-pious hagiography has deprived saints of their humanity and turned them into plaster statues whom we could not imitate even if we wanted to and we wouldn't want to.

The process of canonization was developed several hundred years ago to prevent the abuses of canonization by popular acclaim in which many dubious characters were held up for the devotion and the imitation of the faithful. The present process is elaborate and protected by many safeguards (one almost suspects that Rene Descartes designed it, so careful and rigid is it). Unfortunately, it often means the canonization of either the founders of religious orders or people in whom a Pope takes a particular interest and so, while the piety of the canonized saint is not open to question, his or her attractiveness and appeal to the general Catholic laity is. Thus, canonization—once the instrument and stimulus to popular piety, is now utterly isolated from it. Moreover, when the church violates its own process—as it did in the case of St. Maximilian Kolbe—it reduces the whole dynamic to absurdity (and after Kolbe's anti-semitism was discovered, to embarrassment).

We need our saints back and perhaps Mexican-American Catholics, with their tremendous sensitivity to celebration and festival, will help us get them back but in the process, the Vatican and the theologians ought to rethink present methods of canonization.

Andrew M. Greeley

83. Why did the Pope change his mind about the Holy Days of Obligation?

The Pope didn't change his mind, though he is a man given to frequent changes of mind. What he did was rather change the recommendations of the Commission that reformulated the Code of Canon Law. I don't know why he did that: you'd have to ask him yourself, though usually when the present Pope does something which seems strange, one must look to his Polish experience for an explanation. In Poland the church believed its strength in its bitter fight against the Communist Party lay not merely in theological and organizational bases but also in continuity of custom. Hence, many of the changes in custom since the Second Vatican Council have not occurred in Poland. It could well be that the Pope thought that a change in the Holy Days of Obligations would weaken the vitality of Catholicism and diminish the church's political power in places where it is being oppressed. Maybe he was right. It's hard to see what good was accomplished by the abolition of the Friday abstinence rule and it certainly removed an important element in many Catholics' sense of their own identity.

On the other hand, historians are inclined to believe now that the obligation of church attendance imposed by the first Lateran Council was never intended to be one that bound under pain of mortal sin. Moreover, the difficulties in attending Mass on a working day are such that even under the old moral theology, most Catholics would be excused from Holy Day observance.

My own personal opinion (I knew you'd ask) is that we ought to take a lead from the early Christians and "baptize" the secular feasts, many of which have a religious component to them or even religious origins and that these popular feasts ought to become our Holy Days, though there is some built-in conflict between the notion of festival and the notion of obligation. If it's a festival, one would want to go to church, would not one? (That's the way the Hispanic Americans see it, at any rate, and I think they're right.) Thus, such national holidays as Memorial Day, Labor Day, Presidents Day, Thanksgiving could easily become Christian Holy Days and we might even re-Christianize such popular festivals as St. Valentine's Day and St. Patrick's Day, as well as the Octoberfest, Halloween, and the Carnival. (Halloween is the real feast, reaching way back into pre-Christian antiquity. All Saints never quite worked as a replacement for it.) Could not, for example, Labor Day, which is sort of a modern harvest festival, also be Mary's Day in the Harvest Time?

84. Why have we soft-pedaled efforts to convert others to the true faith?

I think we have rather changed the emphasis from convert-making to preaching the gospel (or to use the popular word today, "evangelization"—a word which is popular on the premise that if you use Greek instead of Anglo-Saxon, you make people feel more serious and more learned and more wise and more dedicated.) The "convert-making" mentality often became arrogant, supercilious, chauvinistic and intolerant: we had the truth and the others were wrong, and we had to convert them to the truth by hard-sell persuasion if possible, and occasionally by the sword if necessary. Yet Jesus and his followers did not believe that way at all. They simply preached the good news and welcomed those who were attracted by it. So it must be with us: if our preaching of the gospel and our Christian life attracts others to join us, we welcome them with open arms but we do not go out and high-pressure them to break with their own heritages. Moreover, we ought to remind them that when they become Catholics, they do not forsake their own heritage: they bring it along to share with us. Thus a Baptist who becomes a Catholic also remains a Baptist because the symbols of his religious past accompany him on his pilgrimage even if now he is a formal part of the Catholic Church.

85. Why hasn't the doctrine of limbo been jettisoned?

Gosh, I thought it had. When was the last time you heard anybody talk about limbo in church or in school or in a Catholic textbook? The more appropriate question might be why limbo isn't preached anymore and the answer to that question is that limbo was a theological construct created because the intellectual systems of theologians came into conflict with the gospel teaching of God's mercy and love. Whenever theological ideology and God's love are in conflict, God loses.

The problem began a long time ago when such fathers of the church as St. Augustine over-interpreted the notion that baptism was essential for salvation and that salvation could only occur in and through the Lord Jesus. But, these theologians said, what about the infants who die without baptism? Indeed, what about all those who have never heard of the Lord Jesus?

Augustine was quite capable of assigning such people to the ranks of the damned, thus demonstrating that even one of the greatest minds in history can operate quite stupidly when caught up in the need of an apriori system. Faced with the problem of the universality and the efficaciousness of God's love and the problem of unbaptized infants, Augustine and other early fathers unhesitatingly chose to deny the central theme of the gospel—the universality and the efficaciousness of God's love. So it will always be, one fears, when the system conflicts with the scriptures.

Later theologians tried to hedge their bets: a good and generous and gracious God could not possibly send such infants to hell; but nonetheless, this goodness and graciousness is tied to and captured by human performance and if for one reason or another humans failed to perform the sacrament of baptism for such infants, there was simply no way God could admit them to eternal happiness either. So limbo emerged, never as a doctrine, but as theological explanation. Even as recently as 30 years ago, doctoral dissertations which pointed out that limbo was a medieval construct, scarcely a matter of faith, created enormous controversy at the seminary I attended.

Today both the medieval compromise of limbo and patristic harshness of damning the infants have been dismissed as absurdities—and one might say that it is about time, too. Today we are much more likely to say that God loves everyone and wills the salvation of everyone and how he accomplishes it is his problem, not ours. Patently, this is not an excuse for carelessness in seeking the administration of the sacrament. Rather, it is an assertion that we have no right to impose the limitations of our theological system on his goodness.

86. Why does the hierarchy still cling to such ridiculous and antiquated customs as pointed hats, cassocks, birettas, etc.?

Gosh, I think they're kind of cute, don't you? Why do judges and professors wear robes, why do people dress up in black and white ties for formal occasions, why do women spend considerable amounts of money before they attend a fancy dress ball? The answer is that there are certain events and activities which seem to be so important and so solemn that we dress in different and special clothes for them. The borderline between the solemn and the ridiculous, between the playful and the absurd is often very thin (as the great book *Homo Ludens* pointed out long ago). Ceremony, ritual, and elaborate costume can create dignity and solemnity and can also make us look like plain damned fools. I personally think it should be great fun to be a Monsignor or even a Cardinal, not because of the power and the prestige and certainly not for the income, but rather because I think the colors of the robes of both non-sacramental ecclesiastical career rewards are enormously colorful and great fun: they sure do beat the drab clothes that bankers, business men and college professors wear. Of course, if I were a Cardinal I would require two accolytes to serve and a cross-bearer to precede me as I march across the University campus every morning, sprinkling holy water as I go.

Andrew M. Greeley

The Catholic Church may have its deficiencies as a church nowadays, but it's still great theater and I doubt that we will improve our quality as church by eliminating the theater.

I wear the Roman collar and clerical black on public occasions (like lectures and television programs) not because I take their basic symbolism seriously (the black stands for death when Christianity stands for life) but because in the popular symbolism the Roman collar and the black suit stand for priest and that, for the Catholic people is thought to be extremely important. Mind you, I don't criticize priests who appear in such public situations in other garb. I merely say it's insane to lose the symbolism, even if it's a derivative and inadequate and in some fashion inaccurate symbolism.

87. Why is it necessary for humankind to be redeemed?

"Redemption" is one of the finest examples I know of a story term being turned into a theological concept and being perverted and misunderstood in the process. Redemption initially meant either the ransoming of a captive or the buying of a slave to set the slave free. It was a word filled with powerful narrative connotation, rich with a sense of the new life of freedom and community that the followers of Jesus experienced in his death and resurrection. In searching for a story image, for a metaphor, if you will, which would convey the nuances, the emotional overtones of deep meaning of this experience, they said, in effect, well, it's something like what happened when a captive is ransomed or a slave is liberated.

Fair enough, so long as one realizes that one is dealing with poetry, image, story. But if one converts this story term which is designed from experiential and emotional images into a hyper-rationalized concept then one misses the whole point and ends up saying really crazy things like the blood of Jesus was the price the Heavenly Father demanded to forgive human sin. Obviously such a notion is an absurdity but it comes from mixing literary genres, i.e., mixing rational theology (which has a place and a very important place) with poetry and story (which also has an important place and indeed a primordial place).

So to say that humankind needed to be "redeemed" means that humankind needed to be freed from the chains in which it found itself and needed to be reintegrated with the world, with one another, and with God. The need for this kind of "redemption," i.e., a redemption which leads to freedom and communal liberation and de-alienation, is as obvious as anything can be. It is in the nature of human experience as we often enough undergo it that we sense that we are both imprisoned and alienated. The life, death and resurrection of Jesus are designed to show us the way to break free from alienation and imprisonment and by showing us actually begin the process of liberation and de-alienation, the process of communion and freedom.

The question of what it is that alienates us and imprisons us is the same question as to what original sin is and that is a question beyond the scope of the present volume (though I would refer you to my book, *The Bottom Line Catechism*, also published by The Thomas More Press, in which I discuss the matter at great length). In response to the present question, however, it is sufficient that humankind needs to be redeemed, not because of some extrinsic price that God has imposed on us but rather because of the fractured, alienated and imprisoned condition in which unquestionably and indubitably we find ourselves.

88. Why didn't the church make a strong and universal condemnation of Hitler's persecution of the Jews?

Pius XII was, as noted in the answer to the previous question, an erratic, indecisive and vacillating man. Several times he prepared such condemnations and then backed off from them, in part because he was afraid of greater persecution of the church if he should take on Hitler directly and in part because he was afraid, and not without reason, of greater persecution of the Jews. He was deeply influenced by the fact that when the Dutch Bishops condemned Nazi atrocities against Jews, the Germans responded by killing even more Jews, 40,000 more according to some estimates. Pius was afraid that even worse would happen if he spoke out. He may well have been wrong, both morally and prudentially, but there doesn't seem to be much reason to question the good faith of his decision. History will doubtless be very harsh on him and it is certainly not necessary for Catholics to feel that they have to defend his indecisiveness. On the other hand, hindsight wisdom and courage are easy virtues and Pius' hesitation, if not excusable, is at least understandable, given his time, his place and his personality.